MURDER
& CRIME

STIRLING

MURDER & CRIME

STIRLING

Lynne Wilson

First published 2012

The History Press
The Mill, Brimscombe Port
Stroud, Gloucestershire, GL5 2QG
www.thehistorypress.co.uk

British Library Cataloguing in Publication Data.
A catalogue record for this book is available from the British Library.

ISBN 978 0 7524 6272 1

Typesetting and origination by The History Press
Printed in Great Britain
Manufacturing managed by Jellyfish Print Solutions Ltd

Contents

About the Author

Lynne Wilson is the creator and editor of www.scotlandshistoryuncovered.com. Although Lynne's career has mainly consisted of scientific and research work, she has always had a strong interest in the social history of the Victorian era, spending many years researching this topic. Having previously studied in both Edinburgh and Glasgow, Lynne now lives in Stirling and writes about the history of these cities in her spare time.

Acknowledgements

I would like to thank the following organisations for their assistance in this book project:

The National Library of Scotland
The British Library
Stirling Central Library
The *Scotsman*
The *Glasgow Herald*
The National Archives of Scotland
The Scottish Prison Service

Introduction

Scotland's former capital city and medieval Royal Burgh, Stirling, has been the focal point in Scotland's history throughout the ages, and, equally, integral in shaping the future of the country. The battles of Stirling Bridge and Bannockburn have been well documented and are familiar to many, however, leaving this 'Braveheart' image of Stirling aside, the social history of this city from the early 1800s to the early 1900s contains just as much intrigue, with plenty of examples of dark deeds and macabre tales.

The Black Boy Fountain, built in the mid nineteenth century, commemorates those who died in Stirling from the plague. (Author's collection)

The dark streets around the Old Town lent themselves well to criminals and evil-doers at the end of the eighteenth century and start of the nineteenth century, with the town only gaining gas street lighting in 1826. Like many British towns, Stirling experienced a great population surge due to the Industrial Revolution in the nineteenth century, and suffered from overcrowding and unsanitary conditions. As an established market town, farmers would come from all around to sell their products in Stirling, with the Mercat Cross in Broad Street being the centre of the town's trading activity. Next to the Cross in Broad Street stood the Tolbooth, still in use today as an entertainments venue. The Tolbooth, built in the early eighteenth century, functioned as a courthouse and prison.

Overcapacity and filthy for a great many years, the Tolbooth was finally replaced in 1847 by a new town jail, following pressure from reformers keen to improve prison conditions throughout the country.

A modern police force was still ten years away at this point however, and a purpose-built Sheriff Court was not completed until 1864. Broad Street, in the Old Town, was at the centre of town life as well as trading in the late eighteenth century, with the top of the town near the castle being host to grand houses in Castle Wynd and the Holy Rude. Broad Street itself was mainly home to rich merchants and down the hill from this area, the poorer houses were situated. This area at the top of the town was bustling with people from all walks of life and trades. Running parallel to Broad Street, St John Street was where the flesh market was situated, with fleshers slaughtering animals on the streets.

With the opening of the railway line to Stirling from Glasgow and Edinburgh, however, the bottom part of the town established itself as the new commercial centre.

The railway also brought wealthy commuters to Stirling, leading to the development of the King's Park area, whilst all the time the Old Town, which was left to the poorest inhabitants, became more run down and overcrowded.

Following an outbreak of cholera in 1832, however, sewers were constructed under the streets and spacious new housing areas were created to the east of the Old Town to help alleviate the congestion. Many new developments also came in the latter part of the nineteenth century, with Stirling gaining an infirmary in 1874; the building which housed it still standing in Spittal Street. In the same year, horse-drawn trams also came to Stirling and the Smith Art Gallery and Museum opened. All things considered, the town was shaping up to be a place of culture and modernity; however, the social problems in the more

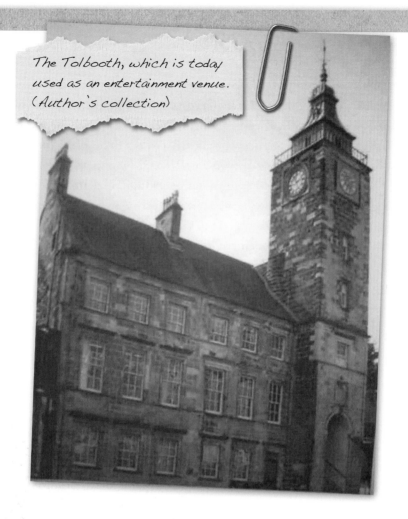

The Tolbooth, which is today used as an entertainment venue. (Author's collection)

deprived areas of Stirling, the same which existed in all towns and cities at the time, created a breeding ground for crime. By the early twentieth century, the top of the town was still poverty ridden and suffered from overcrowding. The solution to the problem only came after the First World War, when many of the slum dwellings were finally cleared and replaced with more modern and sanitary accommodation. These slum clearances continued up until the 1950s, replacing many of the buildings in Baker Street, Broad Street and St John Street.

This book focuses on the period between the early 1800s until the 1930s, a time during which the social problems of overcrowding and poverty described above went hand-in-hand with murder and crime. The nineteenth century saw many changes in the way crime was dealt with in Scotland. Scottish burghs were given power in 1833 to establish police forces if they had not already done so. Around this time, the Police Courts dealt with the minor offences, which would usually result in a fine or a short sentence, and this court dealt only with Summary Procedure, where the case was heard without a jury being present. Any cases which were thought to require a harsher sentence than the Police Court could give were remitted to a higher court. A great many minor offences appeared before the police, however it was often noted during the latter half of the nineteenth century that with the improvements in policing and street lighting, these types of crimes, such as theft or common assault, were committed far less than at the start of the century. However, as better policing led to more crimes being detected and consequently brought to court, along with better press reporting, it must have seemed to the inhabitants of Stirling that the reverse was in fact true. Apart from the obvious reasons of poverty and destitution, the authorities also looked for other trends in the occurrence of petty crimes, with one report in 1838 on the state of crime finding that:

Barnton Street, which replaced Broad Street as the commercial centre of the town in the mid-nineteenth century. (Author's collection)

Crime appears to be not only hereditary to a considerable extent, but also in some degree to belong to particular occupations. Thus I find that Carters, as a class, are more addicted to stealing than people following most other employments; the stolen articles consisting generally of farm produce, coals etc, which they have many opportunities of taking, and for which they have a ready consumption; the hay and corn thus obtained, enabling them to spend in drink, money which must otherwise have gone to buy food for their horses. Wandering tinkers have earned so bad a reputation in Scotland, that their name is now almost synonymous with 'thief'. Not only in these cases, but as a general rule, I have found that those who are in the habit of moving from place to place, commit an undue share of the offences; though doubtless, there is a mixture of cause and effect in this, one reason of persons quitting one place of abode after another, being that they have committed offences and fallen under suspicion. Colliers and fishermen I have often found, as classes, to be in the frequent practice of committing assaults and other breaches of the peace (generally from drunkenness), but to be for the most part honest.

The Sheriff Court dealt with the majority of criminal and civil cases, however, as the power of this court was limited, major crimes were usually remitted to the High Court and civil cases, which were of a more complex nature, were usually dealt with by the Court of Session in Edinburgh. As with the Police Court, the Sheriff Court could deal with cases under Summary Procedure, but in addition its sentencing power was greater. The Sheriff Court also dealt with cases under the more serious Solemn Procedure, where the cases were heard by a Sheriff sitting with a jury. Any cases thought to be out with the sentencing scope of the Sheriff Court were remitted to the High Court. As the only High Court of Justiciary was in Edinburgh, the 'Circuit Court of Justiciary' would often be set up in the Sheriff Courts of the towns in Scotland in order that serious crimes could be tried in the local area.

High Court or Circuit Court trials were held before a judge and jury, and could give very lengthy prison sentences or even the death penalty.

With many any high profile murders taking place during the time period covered in this book, the result was often public execution of the criminals. These public executions, in the form of hangings, were carried out in front of the courthouse in Broad Street. Drawing large crowds of spectators, these executions were seen by some as entertainment, therefore many people were glad when they were eventually replaced by executions inside prisons in 1868.

Stirling during this period, however, did not have its own executioner. The last town executioner, John (or Jock) Rankine, had performed the task up until 1771, when he was removed from office. There had been many complaints about his conduct, with reports of him being unable to perform his duties and of 'keeping a bad house in the night time', by disturbing the neighbours and entertaining people of bad character. It is reported that Rankine died after choking on a chicken bone which had been left in soup prepared by his often ill-treated wife. After the removal of Jock Rankine, executions in Stirling were carried out by hangmen from other towns. John Murdoch, the hangman of Glasgow, was one such executioner whose services were often utilised. Murdoch began the job of hangman in 1831, at which time he was well into his sixties. Having carried out his last execution around twenty years later, he was the oldest hangman Britain had known.

Lynne Wilson, 2012

Case One

Wife Murder

The Execution of Allan Mair, 1843

Suspect: Allan Mair
Age: 80
Charge: Murder
Sentence: Execution

EXECUTION

Of Allan Mair, an old man of 80, for the Murder of Mary Fletcher, aged 85, at Candie End, or Curshort, parish of Muiravonside, who suffered at Stirling, this morning, Oct. 4, 1843, together with his behaviour in the Condemned Cell.

A newspaper clipping detailing the execution of Allan Mair. (Courtesy of The Scotsman Archives)

Eighty-year-old Allan Mair underwent the spectacle of a public execution on 4 October 1843 for the murder of his eighty-five-year-old wife, Mary. As usual, a large crowd turned out to witness the event. Being placed upon the drop, he was accommodated with a chair due to his age, which he was no sooner seated upon when he embarked upon a speech to the crowd. This speech, which lasted ten minutes, consisted of Mair haranguing the crowd in an angry, animated fashion, described by one newspaper as 'hurling fire and brimstone, death and damnation' on all who had any part in his apprehension and trial. Still denying his guilt, Mair insisted that he had been the victim of lies and, during his trial, and had been prevented from calling such witnesses or bringing papers with him that might prove his innocence. Once his speech was finished, prayers were said for him and the cap and rope were adjusted by the executioner in preparation. At this point Mair 'gave audible vent to his pent up feelings' by wishing that all involved in the case 'be sent to destruction' immediately after his death.

Mair had earlier refused the customary glass of wine offered to those about to be hanged in order to steady their nerves, stating that he wanted no such help to take him through the scene that was before him. When the signal was given, the drop fell and Mair should have been killed instantly, however, as he was so frail, his neck did not snap, and instead he was slowly strangled. It has been reported that the hangman, a young medical student who had stood in for the usual executioner, had to get hold of Mair's legs and swing upon them to add the extra weight required to break the neck.

Mair had been convicted of murdering his wife, Mary, by beating her with a stick. The *Stirling Advertiser* reported that a quarrel had arisen between Mair and his wife in their home at Avonbridge on the night of 14 May 1843 over some trivial matter. Mair had then proceeded to swear at Mary and beat her on the head, arms and chest with a large stick. Neighbours, hearing her cries, went to assist, but Mair, known to be a violent man who possessed firearms, threatened to shoot anyone who came near. The next morning, when word of the assault reached the police, they came to the house and found Mary to be very ill in bed. Mair was then taken into custody, on a charge of assault. However, by the time he was examined before the Sheriff, Mary had died from her injuries. Mair was therefore fully committed to Stirling Jail on a charge of murder.

Allan Mair's trial was heard in the Stirling Circuit Court, beginning with evidence from a witness named Helen Bennie, a neighbour who gave evidence that she was a regular visitor to their home and was with Mary when she died. Helen told the court that Mary could not walk well, having hurt her back, and that Mair was often abusive to her and would deprive her of food. Additionally, a few weeks before the incident, she told the court that she had seen Mair strike Mary with a spade. Helen stated that she and other neighbours often had to provide Mary with food, which they did when Mair was out of the house. On 14 May, at around seven o'clock in the evening, Helen saw Mary when she gave her some supper. Later she heard cries and the sound of blows being struck, with Mary's voice saying, 'Let me lie and die in peace, and don't strike me any more'. Mair was then heard

A nineteenth-century box bed. (© Wolfgang Sauber)

to say that he would leave her alone if she 'put in the sneck of the bed', in other words to lock the wooden doors of the box bed in which she lay. Mary had been heard telling her husband that she could not do this as she couldn't see, but Mair replied, 'I will make you glad to put in the sneck', and proceeded to beat her again. The next morning Helen went to see Mary and found her crouched at the foot of the bed, wearing a cap and an old piece of cotton cloth around her shoulders, with her shirt covered in blood and a great deal of blood on the bed. Mair was complaining that he had gotten no sleep due to Mary banging on the locked wooden doors of the bed. Helen told the court that she handed some tea to Mary, who took it in her left hand as she could not lift her right hand due to her injuries. Pointing at Mair, she told Helen that he had given her the bruises, at which point Helen sent for a police officer and Mair was taken into custody. The jury brought a unanimous verdict of guilty and Mair was sentenced to death.

After the trial, Mair had been determined to refuse food in order to end his life, managing to abstain from food for four days. However, his appetite proved too strong in the end and he began eating the food supplied to him in prison. Having received daily visits by the prison chaplain and several other ministers, Mair had become optimistic – having heard that a petition from the Provost and the Magistrates had been given to the Secretary of State for the Home Department in an attempt to have the death sentence commuted due to Mair's age. An attempt, however, which proved to be in vain.

SOLVED

Child Murder

The Case of Noble Dan, 1924

Suspect: Alexander 'Noble Dan' Hannah

Charge: Murder and Indecent Assault

Sentence: Detained at Lunatic Asylum

On 20 November 1924, newspapers reported the discovery of the body of a four-year-old female child in a close in Baker Street, in Stirling's town centre. The crime, described as an 'outrage and brutal murder', caused a great deal of media interest.

The young girl, Nessie Reid, was described as 'a bright little girl, with beautiful auburn hair and winsome manners'. She had left her parents' house about seven o'clock the previous evening, being told by her mother to go and fetch her younger brother. However, when she did not return, her parents became increasingly concerned, and, at eleven o'clock, a search commenced in the neighbourhood. All likely places were searched, but it was not until 1.30 a.m. that the grim discovery was made. Mrs Brown, a neighbour of the Reid family, discovered the little girl in a hidden alcove at the end of the close in Baker Street, where she lived. Mrs Brown, who was very upset at the finding, detailed that she had been instructing searchers in a nearby garden when she bumped against an object against the surrounding wall. Reaching down in the darkness with her hand, she was horrified when she realised she was clutching a mass of human hair. Having summoned the others, the child's stiff and cold body was taken to Stirling Royal Infirmary, where she was pronounced dead. The evidence pointed to death caused by strangulation.

Baker Street in Stirling, located in the 'top of the town' area. (Author's collection)

This area at the back of the close was separated by stone walls from neighbouring gardens; thus, the police theorised that the girl's body must have been thrown over the wall from one of those gardens. The girl's aunt, Mrs Bulloch, however, formed a different theory of the events that evening. As the body had been in a sitting position in the corner, she thought the child may have crept there for safety and that the murder must have been committed in the close itself. Another neighbour, James Weldon, had said the close was very frequently used by drunk men coming from public houses in the vicinity.

Nessie's parents had been 'quiet living people', held in high regard by their neighbours. Her father, George Reid, had not been in the best of health since the end of the First World War, but had been employed occasionally as a joiner, earning an honest living. Consequently, the outrage felt by local people was even greater, that such a tragedy should befall this family.

Two men were arrested soon after the murder, but were subsequently released, having been able to answer all questions put to them to the satisfaction of the police. In the meantime, as one of these men was being arrested, a number of women in the town had armed themselves with stones and tried to get to the man, shouting that they would 'lynch him'. Following the release of these two men, the railway authorities in Stirling and Bridge of Allan informed the police of suspicions they had formed regarding a traveller who was going north, and acting in an agitated manner. Police issued a description of the man, known as 'Noble Dan'. Having many aliases, Noble Dan's real name was thought to be Alexander Hannah. He was thirty-two years old, and was described as 'a coarse speaker', with a record of offending in towns throughout Britain; one offence, for instance, was for committing an indecent assault on a girl. Described as being 'addicted to drink', Noble Dan was said to 'tramp about the country living in lodging houses'. Additional suspicion had fallen on him when, in a lodging house in Stirling, one of the other men said, 'I suppose the police know who the murderer is', at which point Noble Dan swiftly got up and abruptly left the lodging house. This, together with a report of him having been seen in the close on the night in question, pointed strongly to Noble Dan being the culprit.

The funeral of little Nessie Reid took place on 21 November – a cold, windy day – at Ballengeich Cemetery. The funeral procession left the house at 48 Baker Street, with the road packed with hundreds of people, who lined the way to the cemetery. Meanwhile, the search went on for Noble Dan, who had been sighted at Banknock and was thought to be heading west. A man fitting his description had been seen crossing over fields in various places, presumably to avoid the roads where he might be apprehended. Two days later, it was reported that an arrest had been made. Noble Dan had called at Whitehill Farm, Gartcosh, and had asked for tea. A farm servant, however, recognising the man from the description that had been circulated by police, quickly informed the local constable.

On being questioned, the man gave his name as 'Bickerstaff', one of the many aliases used by Alexander 'Noble Dan' Hannah. Hannah was then taken by car and handed over to the Stirling Police. On 24 November 1924, Hannah (now being referred to as Bickerstaff) appeared before the magistrate at Stirling Burgh Police Court and was remanded in custody. A week later, he again appeared in the court and the case was remitted to the Sheriff Court. Bickerstaff was said to have 'stood with a strained indifference' during the proceedings. As Bickerstaff had been certified 'insane' several times in the few years preceding the murder, it was decided that he should be examined in order to decide whether he was fit to plead and therefore be put to trial for the crime. A special sitting of the High Court of Justiciary took place in Stirling on 16 March 1925, where it was detailed that Bickerstaff was charged with the murder of Nessie Reid, and additionally of the indecent assault of another girl (aged seven) in a passage at Irvine Place, Stirling.

An inquiry of the accused's psychological condition was then held, with evidence given by two doctors who had previously treated Bickerstaff – describing him as being in a 'state of threatening danger to the lieges'. Another report was given by Dr McRae of the Ayr Asylum, who told the court that Bickerstaff had been under his care two years previously, and had displayed 'a well marked degree of morbid vanity and untruthfulness', which had earned him the nickname of Noble Dan. Dr McRae also said that Bickerstaff had lived the life of 'a vagrant' and had often been drunk, usually on methylated spirits. Dr McRae's opinion was that Bickerstaff had started off as a 'moral degenerate', but his 'irregular mode of life and dissolute habits had caused his mind to undergo definite deterioration'. Prison doctor Dr Garry of Duke Street prison in Glasgow then gave evidence that it was his opinion that Bickerstaff was of 'unsound mind'. Professor Glaister of Glasgow University gave evidence next, detailing four separate examinations where Bickerstaff had answered questions 'promptly and unhesitatingly' but when asked about his past history, Bickerstaff's answers had not always been accurate. Professor Glaister further stated that the accused 'was a person of defective mental calibre, and had at times shown abnormal behaviour', but in his opinion was fit to plead to the charge against him. Dr Henderson of Gartnavel Asylum had also agreed that Bickerstaff was fit to plead, having answered questions 'promptly and to the point' during examinations. Dr McWalter, a prison doctor from Barlinnie Prison in Glasgow, who had previously known Bickerstaff in 1921, told the court that there had been 'nothing abnormal about him' at that time, other than having 'filthy habits and destructive tendencies'. Bickerstaff, however, had later suffered from hallucinations and it had been necessary, stated Dr McWalter, to put him in a padded room in 1923.

At the conclusion of the inquiry, Lord Anderson said that, in view of the fact that the medical evidence was to some extent contradictory, he thought he should publicly state the reasons which led him to a certain conclusion as to the prisoner's present mental capacity, explaining:

The law of Scotland was quite plain to the effect that a prisoner who was insane could not be tried for a crime. And that law was especially applicable to a case of this sort, where one of the two charges made against the prisoner was that he was guilty of the crime of murder. The law indicated that if it was found at the trial of a prisoner that he was insane, he should be detained in an institution suitable for the detention of people who were insane under the jurisdiction of the Prison Commissioners, and at first sight it seemed that there was a certain hardship in that, because it might well be that a person who was quite innocent of the crime or crimes with which he was charged could be incarcerated for a time in one of these criminal establishments. There is little doubt that if a person, whether he was criminally charged or not, was really insane, he must be incarcerated in some institution. Further, when a prisoner who was insane was subjected to the jurisdiction of the Prison Commissioners, he was not treated as a convict – as one who had been convicted of the crimes he was charged with. He was assumed to be innocent of these crimes, according to the fundamental principal of the criminal law, until he had been proved to be guilty.

Lord Anderson proceeded to review the evidence which had been given, coming to the question of whether the accused, even if 'mentally abnormal', was nevertheless fit to plead. Despite the evidence from Professor Glaister and Dr Henderson, His Lordship explained that he was more inclined to listen to the evidence of the other four doctors who had a better knowledge of Bickerstaff's history. Concluding, Lord Anderson said that he was 'clearly satisfied that at the present moment, the accused, Bickerstaff, was insane, unfit to plead and incapable of instructing his defence, and further, could not be tried on these charges'. Bickerstaff was accordingly ordered to be detained during His Majesty's Pleasure. As he was leaving the dock, Bickerstaff gesticulated with his arm and shouted, 'It's a good job the doctors would not testify me in here. I hope that some of the ladies and gentlemen in here will look into this case. I'm as sane as any man here'.

Following these proceedings, Bickerstaff was made an inmate of the Criminal Lunatic Department of Perth Prison. There was a considerable outcry over the judge's decision, however, with many taking the view that Bickerstaff had evaded justice, therefore a movement was started to petition the Secretary for Scotland to reopen proceedings for Bickerstaff to be tried in court.

On 22 October 1925, Bickerstaff was released from the Perth Criminal Lunatic Prison, with his solicitor, Andrew Dewar, receiving a letter from the Crown authorities the previous day, stating:

> With further reference to your letter of the 8th inst., I am desired by the Prison Commissioners to state that the Secretary for Scotland has made an order for the discharge of Alexander Bickerstaff from that department tomorrow about noon. It is understood, however, that arrangements are being made for his apprehension on discharge and for his removal thereafter to Stirling legalised police cells, with a view to his being placed on trial for the crime for which he is at present in custody. You will thus have access to him as a person awaiting trial in Stirling cells.

Bickerstaff arrived in Stirling by train and was taken to the County Buildings, where he was formally charged with the crime. Only a few weeks previously, Bickerstaff had escaped from the lunatic department along with another prisoner, and had been stopped on a lorry at Auchterarder.

Perth Prison, where Bickerstaff was detained as a 'criminal lunatic'. (Author's collection)

On 9 December 1925, a special Circuit Court sat at Stirling. Mr Aitchison, for the defence, began by raising points on the rights of the accused to Lord Murray before he called upon Bickerstaff to plead. Mr Aitchison stated that as Bickerstaff was not lawfully in custody, he could not competently be brought to trial, and moved his Lordship to direct that Bickerstaff be released and be forever free from 'all question or process of the crimes with which he was charged in the indictment'. Mr Aitchison made the point that as Bickerstaff had been committed upon indictment on 9 December 1924, and that he was currently being detained on the same indictment, Bickerstaff was being illegally detained, as the law states that a person can only be detained pending trial for 110 days, and Bickerstaff, at this point, had spend 141 days in custody. Lord Murray, after due consideration, said he 'entertained no doubt that the point which had been brought up for consideration, involved a large constitutional issue, and that it gave rise to questions of considerable difficulty, upon which it would be extremely desirable that an authoritative judgement should be obtained'. Accordingly, he proposed to 'certify for consideration of the High Court, the question of the application of Section 43, and the statutory rights thereby conferred upon the accused'. His Lordship then adjourned the court until the following week for the matter to be taken before a full Bench of the High Court of Justiciary in Edinburgh.

The High Court of Justiciary, however, repelled this plea for liberation and ordered that the trial should proceed, taking place before the end of January 1926. The trial reopened on 18 January in Edinburgh, to a courtroom substantially filled with members of the public. A jury of eight men and seven women were present and witnesses were conveyed to and from Stirling in a designated charabanc. Several of the witnesses were children between the ages of seven and twelve years old. The charge of indecent assault against the seven -year-old girl was heard first.

The first adult witness was Alexander Jeffrey, assistant surveyor of the burgh of Stirling, who detailed the areas in the indictment where the crimes were said to have been committed. In cross-examination by the defence, Mr Jeffrey said that, 'a good many men loafed about Baker Street at night' and that the street was 'a slum at the top half, and there were a number of lodging houses in the vicinity'. The young victim of the assault later gave evidence. She was given a seat near the jury and was questioned by the Lord Advocate. The girl told the court that she had been sent by her mother to buy a box of matches on the evening of 18 November 1924, and at Docherty's Close, a man spoke to her and gave her two pence. Later, after she had gone home, she came out and met the man again, at which time he took her along to Irvine Place, along with another little girl, the man leading her by the hand. When they got to the close, the man said he would give the girl 5s, 'to go to the pictures'. He then took her into the close and sent the other girl off to buy a packet of Woodbines. When the other girl had gone, the man then took the little girl on to his knee and committed the indecent assault upon her. The little girl had been taken to the police station a few days after the assault and had picked out Bickerstaff from a number of photographs she had been shown. Whilst in court, Bickerstaff was asked to stand and the girl turned round and pointed him out as the man who had assaulted her. The girl's mother was next to give evidence, telling the court that she had been told by two other children that her daughter had been in a close in Irvine Place with a man. She had asked her daughter if the man had done anything to her, but at first she had said no, only telling her mother what had happened a few days later. After this, and her father finding money in her pockets, the matter had been reported to the police.

Further child and adult witnesses then gave evidence that they had seen the man and the two girls go into the close in Irvine Place, and all identified Bickerstaff as the man they had seen. Other child witnesses gave evidence of having been approached by Bickerstaff on the night of the incident. Another witness, Walter Rutherford, told the court that on that evening, he had gone round to the back of the close and had seen a man and a young girl standing near the wash house. He took the girl out, and had intended to go back, but on hearing that the police were near, he instead went to inform them of the incident. Unfortunately, however, he was unable to identify the man.

Evidence was then heard on the second charge, that of murder. The victim's mother, Mary Reid, told how her daughter left the house sometime before seven o'clock on the evening of 18 November 1924. Mrs Reid then detailed the events leading up to her daughter being found in the back court in Baker Street. The next witness, Mrs Ritchie, a neighbour, described seeing a drunken man in the area that night, whom she identified as Bickerstaff. Andrew Hamilton, a little boy who also lived in Baker Street, told the court how he had been playing with Nessie Reid that evening, and a man had came up to her and asked her to come into his house. Nessie had gone away with him, being carried on the

A newspaper clipping of the trial of Bickerstaff. (Courtesy of The Scotsman Archives)

man's shoulder. The little boy saw them go towards the back court in Baker Street, and stated that Nessie was crying at the time. The boy had gone to Nessie's house to tell her mother, but finding no one there, he returned to the street again. Another child witness, Jessie McGougan, also described seeing the man and the little girl, with the boy following. Several witnesses who took part in the search were then examined, all of whom had gone into the back court at 48 Baker Street and, due to the darkness, had not found the body of Nessie Reid. It was therefore not established whether the body had been there prior to the start of the search or whether it had been put there at some point while the search was in progress.

Police Sergeant Thomas Moir of Bishopbriggs told the court of the night he went to Littlehill Farm, having been told that Noble Dan had been there. The sergeant had searched the bothy at the farm, and, under the bed sheets which had been used by Bickerstaff, he found some 'stockinette'. Sergeant Moir explained that he did not find the owner of the stockinette at Littlehill. Stirling Police Sergeant David Cooper then gave evidence, detailing the marks he saw upon Nessie's body while she was at the infirmary. The marks on her throat, Sergeant Cooper explained, indicated that her throat had been violently compressed. He also noted that there had been blood elsewhere on her body. Detective Sergeant John Cowie of Stirling then told the court that he had examined the bed in the lodging house where Bickerstaff had slept. No bloodstains were found on the bed clothing, but it was evident that he had slept with his boots on, from the particles of soil discovered on the sheets.

Professor Glaister, the Professor of Forensic Medicine at Glasgow University, then took the witness box, detailing the post-mortem that had been carried out by him and Dr Vost. He described a number of wounds and abrasions on various parts of the body, and had come to the conclusion that the cause of death was asphyxia and shock. The asphyxia, Professor Glaister said, had been caused by compression of the air passages on the throat and sides of the neck by 'some rounded mass', such as a piece of clothing held in the hands of the murderer. A mark had also been found on the girl's voice box, which Glaister thought was likely to have been caused by the pressure of a long, ragged and untrimmed fingernail. He then advised that he had carried out an examination of the accused in Stirling, where he had noted that some of Bickerstaff's fingernails had been 'deformed and claw-like', and were at that time untrimmed. Scrapings had been taken from under Bickerstaff's fingernails and analysis under the microscope had revealed red blood corpuscles from the fingers of each hand. Bloodstains had also been found on his jacket, which, in the Professor's opinion, had been washed or wiped with a wet cloth.

Dr Vost also gave evidence, stating that having examined the body of Nessie Reid in Stirling Infirmary at 1.45 a.m., he was of the opinion that she had been dead for not less than five or six hours at that point.

Evidence for the defence was then heard, with only three witnesses being called. The first two witnesses were men who had occupied beds at the lodging house and told the court that Bickerstaff had gone to bed at about 10.20 p.m. that evening. The third witness for the defence was a draper named Lawrence Smith, who lived at 52 Baker Street. Mr Smith explained that on the night of the murder, at approximately 11.30 p.m., he had gone in company with Constable Herbert and had searched the back court at No. 52. Whilst doing so, Constable Herbert had leaned over the dividing wall into the back court of No. 48 and shone his torch around. Mr Smith said that at this point the the corner where the body was later found had been illuminated and he could see clearly that no body was there at that time.

The Old Stirling Infirmary in Spittal Street, where the body of Nessie Reid would have been taken for examination. (Author's collection)

At the conclusion of the evidence, Mr Aitchison for the defence gave his closing speech, in which he said that:

No tribunal dare convict a prisoner upon a charge of the second kind described in the indictment, unless upon the clearest and most conclusive testimony. The presumption of innocence was not a mere fiction in the law of Scotland; on the contrary the presumption of innocence was a cardinal principal of our criminal jurisprudence. Let the jury remember that suspicion was not proof.

He also said that if the jury acquitted the prisoner then 'many people would be bitterly disappointed – people who knew little of mercy and less of justice' and that on the other hand, if they acquitted the prisoner, then 'there would be many thinking, just people glad that in this case they as a jury had the courage and the strength to return a verdict in accordance with conscience'.

The Lord Justice Clerk then commenced his summing up. He pointed out that much of the evidence by the Crown had been given by children, and that the evidence of a child in cases of indecent assault was often 'more intelligent and

more observant than that which was sometimes given by adults'. His Lordship also advised the jury that despite this, they should bear in mind that children 'were susceptible to tutoring' and therefore they should 'weigh carefully the evidence which had been given by the many children examined in this case'. His Lordship also pointed out that in the second charge, Bickerstaff had not been seen at any time with Nessie Reid, and that after he was alleged to have murdered her, he had then returned to a lodging house of seventy inmates where his clothing, if they were bloodstained, would have been seen by a great number of people.

The jury retired to consider their verdict, returning after an absence of thirty-two minutes. The court rapidly filled with people eager to hear the verdict. The foreman of the jury delivered a verdict of guilty on the first charge, that of indecent assault; and not proven on the second charge, that of the murder of Nessie Reid. The 'Not Proven' verdict is an acquittal used only in Scottish law, and is given when the judge or jury does not have enough evidence to convict but is not sufficiently convinced of the defendant's innocence to bring in a not guilty verdict. Sentencing Bickerstaff, Lord Justice Clerk said:

You have been convicted by a discriminating verdict of the jury and after a patient trial, of the crime of indecent assault. That crime has assumed alarming proportions in recent times, and there are indications from the evidence in this case that Stirling is not exempt from its prevalence. You have been already convicted of the same crime, and you were sentenced on the 27 March 1923 to fifteen months' imprisonment for your offence on that occasion. The sentence of the court in this case, is that you be detained in penal servitude for four years.

High Treason

The Execution of Andrew Hardie and John Baird, 1820

Suspects:	Andrew Hardie and John Baird
Age:	27 and 37
Charge:	High Treason
Sentence:	Execution

On a scaffold erected in front of the courthouse in Broad Street, Andrew Hardie and John Baird were executed on 8 September 1820, having been convicted of high treason. At about half past ten the previous night, work had commenced to erect the scaffold. Two coffins, containing sawdust, one bearing the inscription 'Andrew Hardie, aged 27', the other 'John Baird, aged 37', were placed upon it. A board, covering about a third of the coffin, was placed to support the body; a square tub, in which was a considerable quantity of sawdust, was placed at the head of each coffin; to that side of the tub nearest the coffin, a block was fixed. A troop of the 7th Dragoon Guards arrived at about eleven o'clock from Falkirk, and proceeded by the back streets to the castle. Since their conviction, the men had paid very great attention to religion, as was common with prisoners facing the last sentence of the law. Baird had detailed his feelings and hopes to his family, asking them not to mourn for his death, but give thanks to God on his account, stressing the importance of living a good life.

The night before their execution, a few of Hardie's relatives and a brother of Baird's had been permitted to remain with them until the morning. Most of the night was spent reading the scriptures, in prayer, and singing hymns. Since their trial, the two men had been held in Stirling Castle, as it was deemed that the

Stirling Castle. (Author's collection)

Tolbooth, which was the usual place of imprisonment at this time, was not secure enough for such high profile prisoners.

At about one o'clock in the afternoon, the men left their cell and got into the cart which was to transport them to the place of execution in Broad Street. The headsman, with the axe in his hand, took the seat opposite them. Hardie leaned forward and looked into the headsman's face in an attempt to see if he knew him, then remarked to Mr Bruce, the clergyman, that he thought the man was young, aged about twenty. Mr Bruce replied, 'What a painful task for such a young man'. The procession began to move and the men sang one last hymn until they reached the front of the jail. The scaffold was surrounded on all sides by soldiers, the infantry in front, supported by the cavalry. The shops in Broad Street were closed, but the windows were crowded with spectators. Around 6,000 were thought to have assembled in Broad Street to witness the melancholy event. About twenty minutes before two o'clock, the cart halted in front of the scaffold and Hardie got up, placed his right hand on his chest, raised his eyes to the scaffold and exclaimed 'Hail! Harbinger of eternal rest'. The men made their way up the steps and into the courtroom, where prayers were given for them. Afterwards Hardie asked for a glass of wine, and on its being presented to him, he raised the glass towards his mouth and exclaimed, 'A speedy deliverance to my afflicted country', and, on catching the eye of the Sheriff, stated:

> My Lord Sheriff, I beg to return you my fervent thanks for the kind and benevolent attention which you have shown to me and my friends, and the humane attention which you paid in gratifying our wishes on all occasions.

He added that he wished well to the town and Magistrates of Stirling. Baird, then bowing, addressed himself to the Sheriff and expressed similar sentiments. When the time came, they advanced with unfaltering steps to the scaffold. Once there, they both requested to address the assembled crowd. After some discussion with the Sheriff, this was allowed, with the men being reminded that no political address would be permitted. Baird spoke first with the following words:

> Friends and Countrymen! I dare say you will expect me to say something to you of the cause which has bought me here; but on that I do not mean to say much, only that what I have hitherto done, the matter that brought me here was for the cause of truth and justice; of this I have little to say, only that I never gave my assent to anything inconsistent with truth and justice. What I would wish particularly to direct your and my attention to, is to that God who is the judge of all mankind, and all human actions, and to Jesus Christ, the saviour of them. I have never hurt anyone – I have always led an innocent life – and as that is well known to them who know me, I shall say no more about it. I am not afraid of the appearance of the scaffold, or of a mangled body – when I think of the innocent Jesus, whose living body was nailed to a cross, and whose wounds I have often made to bleed afresh by my sins, and through whose merits I hope for forgiveness.

Hardie addressed the crowd next, also speaking of what had brought him there and with a loud voice, said, 'I declare before my God I believe I die a martyr in the cause of truth and justice'. No sooner was this uttered than a person, described as being 'connected with pick pockets', shouted, 'Amen!'. The executioner stepped forward and adjusted the ropes, during which time the two men were fervently praying. At eleven minutes before three o'clock, Hardie, having with his left hand seized the right hand of Baird, dropped the handkerchief, signalling that they were ready. It was observed that there was not much of a struggle when they dropped and their bodies, after hanging for half an hour, were cut down and placed on their coffins, with the face downwards, the neck resting on the block and the head hanging into the tub. The headsman now came to perform his duty, wearing a black veil over his face, a black gown and a cap. On his appearance, a shudder seemed to pass over the crowd, and cries of 'Murder! Murder!' were heard. Three strokes of the axe were required to sever the head of Hardie from the body. The headsman then held up the head with both hands and exclaimed, 'This is the head of a traitor!' He decapitated Baird with two strokes, holding up the head in the same manner. Having performed his duty, the headsman was heard to say, 'I wish to God I had not had it to do'. The bodies were interred in the burial ground of the High Church at nine o'clock the same night, where they lay for many years until they were disinterred and re-buried in Sighthill Cemetery in the north of Glasgow.

People at this time enjoyed a good hanging; in fact, hangings were normally scheduled on Stirling's market days, which usually ensured the attendance of a large crowd. However, this execution had been very controversial due to the

Sighthill Cemetery in Glasgow: the burial site for the bodies of Andrew Hardie and John Baird. (Author's collection)

The headsman's cloak and axe used in the execution of Hardie and Baird. These items are displayed at the Smith Art Gallery and Museum, Stirling. (Author's collection)

beheading which had followed the hanging. Beheading was a punishment for high treason, a charge which had no basis in Scots law, therefore the people thought this part to be barbaric. As the hangman had refused to carry out this part of the sentence, it was reported that the beheading was carried out by a young medical student.

The conviction of people for high treason around this time was a government reaction which sought to deal with men like Baird and Hardie, who were fighting for the rights of the people to be paid a reasonable working wage, in order to support their families. At a time of poverty and unemployment, with slum housing conditions, many were unhappy at the political system, leading to groups of men rising up against the government. The Industrial Revolution brought major changes in agriculture, manufacturing, mining, transportation, and technology, with the introduction of machines that could be operated by cheap, relatively unskilled labour, resulting in the loss of jobs for many skilled manual workers. Many of these unemployed men had been soldiers who had fought in the Napoleonic War, and who were not prepared to accept a lack of income and squalid living conditions. This resulted in the Radical Reform Movement, which eventually took hold across the country. The Government, however, saw the protest of these men as treason. Baird and Hardie had been part of a group which had planned to steal weaponry from the Carron Company, a large manufacturer of cannons a few miles from Stirling, in preparation for a rebellion. However, the group was intercepted at nearby Bonnybridge, where Baird and Hardie were

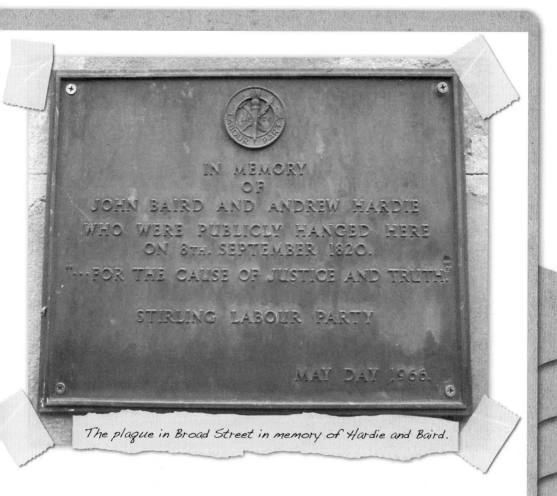

The plague in Broad Street in memory of Hardie and Baird.

captured. Sentenced originally to be hanged, drawn and quartered, this was later commuted to their being hanged and beheaded.

The unpopular trial of these men was followed with great interest by people throughout the country. On 23 June 1820, the Lords Commissioners proceeded to the courthouse in Stirling, escorted by a detachment of the 33rd Regiment. The Grand Jury were sworn in, then addressed by the Lord President Hope, who gave a speech defining the law of treason as applicable to the cases about to come before the court. He concluded by warning the jury that whatever they might have seen or heard regarding treasonable practices, they were to 'lay altogether aside any prejudice or prepossession' and 'be directed in their judgement solely by the evidence laid before them'. The names of those accused of treason were then read out in the court and the prisoners were brought down from the castle under a military guard and placed at the Bar. Eighteen men in total were accused of treason, Baird and Hardie amongst them. The men were informed that 'true bills' had been found against them for high treason.

On 13 July in Stirling, the court met at nine o'clock in the presence of the Lord President, the Lord Justice Clerk, the Lord Chief Baron, the Lord Chief Commissioner and Lord Gillies. The court had been crowded on this day, so much so that there was initially no room for the jury, and the court had to order all those not officially cited to leave, in order that the jury could be accommodated in the courtroom. All eighteen prisoners were again placed at the Bar. Andrew Hardie had been the first of the men to face proceedings, and his indictment was read to the court. The Lord Advocate then opened the case by giving a speech to the jury. Thirteen witnesses were examined in the course of the trial, and after all evidence had been heard, the jury was addressed by Mr Jeffrey, counsel for Hardie, and the Solicitor General, for the Crown. After retiring for around fifteen minutes, the jury returned a guilty verdict.

The following day, the court met at ten o'clock, and the trial of John Baird proceeded. After a full day of evidence, the jury delivered a verdict of guilty of 'Levying war against the King' on Baird the following morning at half past two.

However, on 4 August 1820, a Special Commission took place in the courtroom in Stirling again, with two additional men about to be tried for the same crimes. On this occasion though, the men were given the option to change their original pleas to guilty in order that they may be shown some mercy by the court. Taking this option, their pleas of guilty were then recorded and the two men were acquitted. Baird and Hardie, who were in court for sentencing along with the others convicted of treason, were addressed by the Lord President, who stated:

You present a melancholy spectacle of two and twenty subjects of this country who have forfeited their lives to its justice; a spectacle, I believe, unexampled in the history of this country, such at least as I never witnessed, and I trust in God shall never witness again. The crime of which you have been convicted is the crime of high treason, a crime [of] the highest known to the law [...], whatever may be the motive which a man has in view who engages in the crime of high treason, we all must be aware that the crime, whether ultimately successful or not in its progress, if progress it has, must produce unutterable misery and confusion. It is impossible that treason can make any progress towards success, without deluging the country in which it takes place, in blood and slaughter, in plunder and devastation. In regard to you, Andrew Hardie and John Baird, I can hold out little or no hopes of mercy. You were selected for trial as the leaders of that band in which you were associated. You were convicted after a full and a fair trial; and it is utterly impossible to suppose, considering the convulsions into which this country was thrown, that the Crown must not feel a necessity of making some terrible examples, and as you were the leaders, I am afraid that example must be given by you […] The sentence of the law is – that you and each of you be taken to the place from whence you came, and that you be drawn of a hurdle to the place of execution, and there be hung by the neck until you are dead, and afterwards your head severed from your body, and your body divided into four quarters, to be disposed of as his Majesty may direct – and may God in his infinite goodness have mercy on your souls.

The prisoners were then taken from the Bar. All of them later had their sentences commuted to transportation for life, except Hardie and Baird.

A letter written by William Hardie in Stirling Castle a few days prior to his execution appeared in the *Glasgow Gazette* in 1859, which detailed his part along with John Baird's in the Battle of Bonnymuir:

On the 4th of April, 1820 (the night I left Glasgow with two men, whose names I forbear to mention), we arrived at Germiston, where we found, as was expected, a number of men in arms, whom I immediately joined; and after some delay, expecting some more, as we were told, from Anderston, and other places (but which did not come forward), we got notice where we were to go, and received a very encouraging address from a man I did not know. I was made to understand the nature of our affair by the two men and likewise, that the whole city would be in arms in the course of an hour afterwards, which he who addressed us told us likewise; and that the coach would not be in the following morning; and that England was all in arms, from London downwards, and everything was going on beyond our most sanguine expectations; and declared that there were no soldiers to oppose us betwixt that and Edinburgh; and further, that the whole country was ready to receive us, and well armed; and those that wanted would get arms by the road, refreshments, and everything necessary. I heard likewise, through the course of the day, or early in the evening, that there was going to be a turnout, but I did not get information of the nature of it before our departure. I asked if there was no person going along with us who had instructions how to proceed, or take the charge of us. There was one, Keane, told me that there was a person with us who would give us every satisfaction, but that I might take the command until we came to Condorrat, where we would be joined by a party of fifty or sixty men, and get one there to take the command of the whole; but this I did not assume until we came within a mile of Condorrat, when we halted, and proposed to form ourselves in regular order, and I was appointed by the men themselves to do this, which I did by forming a front and rear rank, and

The house in Condorrat village, where John Baird was born. Condorrat was a a former weaving community. (Courtesy of www.geograph.org.uk)

sized them accordingly, and numbered them the same as a guard; my reason fordoing this was, as we were all strangers to one another, and did not know our names, that if anything were wasted, we might answer to our numbers.

After this was done, I left the party and went before then (with Keane) to find Mr, Baird; and when we found him, there was one, King had been waiting with him upon us coming forward. This King belongs to Glasgow, but what he is I do not know; but this I know, that he acted a very unbecoming part with us. King had told Baird that there was a party of two hundred, well-armed men coming out, and that they were all old soldiers.

After we left Condorrat, our first halt was at Castlecarry Bridge, where we received half a bottle of porter and a penny worth of bread each man, which was paid for, and a receipt obtained for the same. We again proceeded; but I should have observed before this, that King left us at Condorrat, and went before us on the pretext of getting the Camelon and Falkirk people ready by the time we should be forward; and in case we should miss them, or the party that was to meet us, I, with the other four or five stout men, went by the road, and the main party went by the canal bank […]. We proceeded along the road about a mile and a half past Bonnybridge, where we got a signal from the party on the bank to join them, for King had come to them and said that he should have to go up to the moor and wait there until we got a reinforcement from Camelon.

The whole of us turned and went through an aqueduct bridge, and went up about a mile into the moor, and we sat down on the top of a hill and rested (I think) about an hour, when the Cavalry made their appearance; upon this we started upon our feet, and at once resolved to meet them. I proposed forming a square where we were, but Mr. Baird said it would be much better to go under cover of a dyke, which was not far distant; we then immediately ran down the hill, cheering, and took up our position. There was a slap in the dyke, which we filled with pikemen. The Cavalry took a circular course through the moor, and came under the cover of a wood at our right flank. As soon as they made their appearance past the end of the wood, firing commenced immediately. They came up nigh to the dyke – the

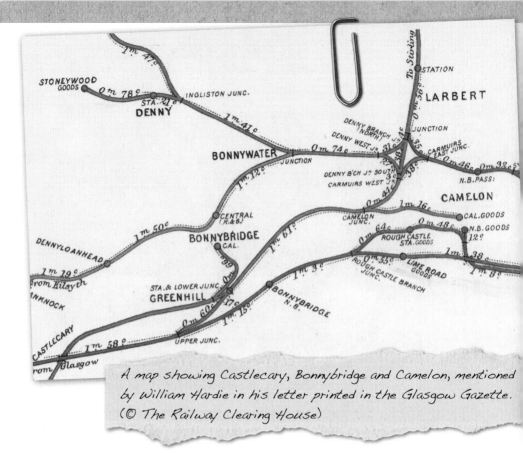

A map showing Castlecary, Bonnybridge and Camelon, mentioned by William Hardie in his letter printed in the Glasgow Gazette. (© The Railway Clearing House)

Hussars in front, led by their officer (Lieutenant Hodgson), who called out to us to lay down our arms, but this was not agreed to. After firing some shots at us, they made an attack at the slap, and got through, but we were repulsed and driven back. They in general, stood a little distance from the dyke, so that our pikes were rendered unserviceable. One of the hussars came close up to the dyke, a little to the right of where I stood, and one of our party made a stab at him. The hussar fired at him in return, and he fell forward on his face. They made a second attack at the slap, and got through, but were kept at bay in the inside, and the officer again called out to us to surrender, and he would do us no harm, which most of our men took for granted, and threw down their arms and ran. Mr. Baird defended himself in a most gallant manner. After discharging his piece, he presented it at the officer empty, and told him he would do for him, if he did not stand off. The officer then presented his pistol at him, but it flashed and

1 8 2 0

BATTLE
of
BONNYMUIR

ON 5th APRIL, 1820, A BAND OF SCOTS
WORKING CLASS RADICALS FOUGHT
HERE FOR THEIR DEMOCRATIC RIGHTS
AGAINST A TROOP OF HORSE
FROM THE BRITISH ARMY.

THE RADICALS TOOK COVER BEHIND
A FIVE-FOOT HIGH DRY-STANE DYKE,
LOCATED IN THIS FIELD;
LATER KNOWN AS
" THE RADICAL DYKE "

THEY WERE QUICKLY OVER-POWERED
AND TAKEN PRISONER, THEIR TWO
LEADERS - JOHN BAIRD FROM
CONDORRAT AND ANDREW HARDIE
FROM GLASGOW - WERE EXECUTED
AT STIRLING

Memorial stone in Bonnyhill Road to those who were lost in the Battle of Bonnymuir. (Author's collection)

did not go off. Mr. B. then took the butt end of his piece, and struck a private on the left thigh, whereupon the sergeant of the hussars fired at him; Mr. B. then threw his musket from him, and seized a pike, and while the sergeant was in the act of drawing his sword, wounded him in the right arm and side. Before this the officer was wounded in the right hand, and his horse also was wounded; yet, notwithstanding, he would not allow one of his men to do us any harm, and actually kept off, with his own sword, some of the strokes that were aimed against us. One of the hussars recognised one of our party who, he said, had wounded his officer, and would have instantly sabred him, had not the officer speedily interfered, and told him there was too much done already. Although my enemy, I do him nothing but justice by saying that he is a brave and generous man. He came up in front of his men, and I am truly happy (but surprised) that he was not killed, as I know there were several shots fired at him.

After the wounded men, and those who tried to make their escape, were all brought together, we were taken off the moor. Mr. B. and I assisted one of the wounded men, until we got a cart, and they were put into it; one of them w-as dreadfully wounded in the head, I think in four places, and shot through the arm. Another old man, with a frightful looking wound in his face, so much so that his jaw bone was seen perfectly distinct; and the third, with a sabre wound in his head; and two or more left on the field for dead.

It was later established that 'King' who Hardie makes reference to in his letter was a government spy.

Case Four

Murder at Garvel Farm

The Trial of Elizabeth Thomson, 1939

Suspect: Elizabeth Thomson
Charge: Murder
Found: Not Guilty

On 2 August 1939, at a sitting of the High Court at Stirling, Elizabeth Thomson stood trial for the alleged murder of her husband, John Thomson. The charge against her impicated that she had assaulted her husband at their farm in Cambus, near Stirling in May of the same year, by 'striking him several blows on the head with an axe or other similar instrument, and along with a fifteen-year-old boy employed at the farm, discharged both barrels of a loaded shotgun at Thomson and shot him in the left arm and in the face, and did thus murder him'.

Throughout the trial, the farm boy was simply referred to as 'the boy', and there is no record of his name, which presumably is due to his age at the time. At the start of the trial, the defence raised an objection to the competency of the evidence of the farm boy, following a medical examination that had found the boy to be 'feeble minded'. It had been stated by the doctors, however, that although he had the mentality of a boy of between eight and ten years, he *did* know the difference between truth and falsehood. After putting the boy on oath and explaining to him that he would be asked certain questions, and that he must tell the truth and nothing but the truth, Lord Moncrieff allowed the boy's evidence to be heard. The boy proceeded to tell the court that at around half past five in the afternoon on 26 May 1939, Mr Thomson had told him he was

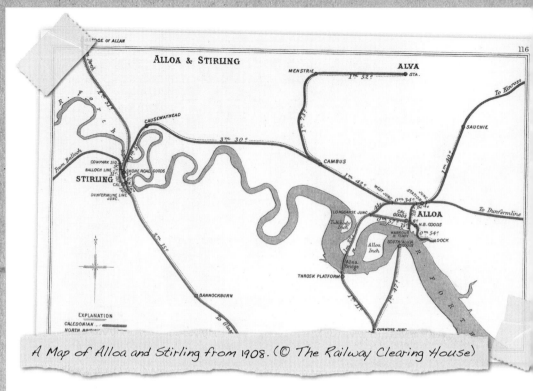

A Map of Alloa and Stirling from 1908. (© The Railway Clearing House)

going to nearby Tullibody to get some tobacco. The boy did not believe this, however, as this was what his employer always said when he was actually going to Stirling town. Mrs Thomson, who had been to Stirling that day, returned to the farm shortly afterwards and gave him sweets. On telling her that Mr Thomson was away again, she replied that he was, in fact, still there and said, 'I wish you could do something to him.' The boy stated that on asking her what she meant by that, Mrs Thomson replied, 'Come along and we will try and do something to him,' and then said, 'Come on and you'll see'. The boy told the court that he and Mrs Thomson then went to the farmhouse, where she took down the gun from the rack above the door. Putting two cartridges in the barrel she said, 'Here, take that,' and handed him the gun. The boy then said that he had asked Mrs Thomson what she was going to do and she replied, 'Wait and you will see'. They then left the farmhouse and went to the bothy, where Mrs Thomson went in for an axe. They then proceeded to the midden, where Mrs Thomson said to him, 'Mind, and try and use the gun'. The boy then told the court that whilst they were at the midden he heard Mr Thomson coming up the road, shouting and swearing. He remarked to Mrs Thomson at the time, 'Listen to that', to which she replied, 'Aye, isn't it awful'. When Mr Thomson came into the farm close, she had asked the boy if he was ready and

Murder at Govel Farm

told him not to be frightened. He then stated that she 'rushed out with the axe and hit him on the head', meaning that Mrs Thomson had struck her husband, at which point Mr Thomson fell to the ground. The boy then told the court that he started crying, but Mrs Thomson had pushed him outside and, after hitting her husband a further two or three times with the axe, said to him, 'Go on son, shoot him now'. He added that she pulled him by the back of his jacket, out to where John Thomson was lying and told him to pull the trigger. The boy stated that at this point he was holding the gun and Mrs Thomson was punching him on the back, when she happened to hit his left hand and his thumb hit the trigger and the shot went off, missing John Thomson. The boy said that Mrs Thomson then called him a 'stupid ass' and told him where to put his finger on the trigger. Pulling the trigger again, he shot Mr Thomson, then let the gun drop and started to cry. He stated that Mrs Thomson then went over to him with two dusters and told him to get things cleaned up. They then cleaned bits of grass where blood had spilled and pulled Mr Thomson into the long grass, taking hold of a leg each. Mrs Thomson then cleaned the gun and the axe with a duster and the boy put some straw over the grass where there were bloodstains. The boy told the court that he then went to the bothy but he could not sleep and he did not undress. Early the next morning, he and Mrs Thomson went to clean up any blood they had missed during the night and Mrs Thomson again cleaned the gun, mentioning the fingerprints. She then gave him the gun after wrapping a cloth around the barrel and told him to take it outside and lay it next to Mr Thomson. She then burned the blankets and told him to change into another shirt so that she could burn the one he was wearing.

The boy went on to say that later, when they went to do the milking, she said to him, 'Remember, this is between me, you and the lamp post. Dead men tell no tales.-' The boy then told the court that he was taken to Alloa by the police for questioning, and admitted that at first he had told them lies to protect Mrs Thomson.

FARMER'S WIDOW ACCUSED OF MURDERING HUSBAND

*A newspaper clipping detailing information on the case of
Elizabeth Thomson. (Courtesy of The Scotsman Archives)*

In a cross-examination by the defence, the boy told the court that he liked to go to the cinema on Saturday nights to see cowboy films, 'where there were guns, horses and shooting'. He was asked if he knew what happened to people who commit murder, to which he replied, 'Yes, they sometimes get fined, and some get so many years and others get hung'. He added that he had been frightened of John Thomson when he was drunk and said that on one occasion, Thomson pulled him out of bed and 'chased him round the place'. The boy also confessed that he 'sometimes told a good many stories to save himself from trouble' and that he had not always been truthful. In addition, he admitted that he could not tell the time, which cast some doubt upon the accuracy of the timing of events he had stated at the start of the trial.

A statement by Mrs Thomson was then read to the court by Inspector Denholm from Alloa. In the statement, she detailed that she was thirty-eight years old, and had been married for seventeen years. She and her husband had no children, and her life had been an unhappy one due to her husband's drinking. She explained that he 'went away on his own, and returned the worse of drink, when he behaved like a madman.' She also said that he had previously assaulted her and she had asked the police for protection against him, and, as a result, he had been warned by the police regarding his conduct. Mrs Thomson further stated that any quarrels they had were always as a result of him being drunk and that all the boys who had been employed on the farm had left, due to fear of her husband, who had previously broken the back door with an axe and threatened her on more than one occasion with a gun. The next part of her statement detailed the events of 26 May:

On Friday, May 26, I left here about one o'clock and went to Stirling to do shopping. I returned about 9 p.m. and went to see if the chickens had been shut up. I then returned to the house and went to bed at 10.25 p.m. I didn't hear a sound all night. I woke about 3 a.m., turned over again, and went to sleep. I sleep with the bed clothes over my head. There was a strong wind blowing. I got up about 5.30 a.m. and wakened the boy in the bothy. I then went out to the byre and commenced milking the cows along with the boy. I then went to the house and made breakfast for the boy, and afterwards I sent him to the stackyard with a calf. He then came to me and let out a roar, 'Where's John Thomson? A body is lying in the field'. I went to the stack yard and saw something lying in the field. I came back to the house, wrote a note to the Tullibody constable, and sent the boy with the note. I then looked for Thomson's gun and it wasn't on the rack above the kitchen door. I went upstairs and looked in Thomson's room and he wasn't there.

Inspector Denholm told the court that following a statement made by the boy, he returned to the farm and charged Mrs Thomson with the murder of her husband. She had replied at the time, 'That is not true'. The Inspector said that there had been no sign of tears or distress on her part at that time.

The following day the trial resumed with Mrs Thomson in the witness box. She told the court that for several years she and her husband had at times occupied separate bedrooms, but, during the last year, it had become a regular thing due to his drunken behaviour. She explained that on the day of the tragedy she had gone to Falkirk to get treatment for a sprained ankle, returning at about ten o'clock. Meeting the boy at the gate, she was told by him that her husband had gone out again for the night. On entering the farmhouse, she did a few odd jobs before going to bed at 10.25 p.m. At half past five, she awoke, having slept all night, and went down to the kitchen, where she lit the kitchen fire and then went out to do the milking with the boy. Mrs Thomson told the court that her husband did not appear that morning, but that this was not an unusual occurrence. A short time later, after breakfast, Mrs Thomson stated that the boy had come in and said that there was a body in the stack yard and he thought it was John. Mrs Thomson was asked in court whether she had been upset on finding her husband dead, to which she replied that she had. She was then asked whether she had struck her husband with an axe or had coerced the boy into shooting him with a gun, to which she answered 'no' to both questions. Mrs Thomson was then asked if she got on with her husband when he was sober, and she replied, 'Perfectly. It was only the drink that caused the trouble.'

The Revd Walter McIntyre then gave evidence on behalf of the accused, telling the court that Mrs Thomson had been a member of his church for sixteen years and that in the early years of her marriage, she and her husband had been very happy. Revd McIntyre explained, however, that in recent years Mrs Thomson had complained of her husband's drunken behaviour and although the Revd had endeavoured to get Mr Thomson to go to church, he never appeared. Revd McIntyre went on to say that on the Sunday after the tragedy, he had visited the farm and had a private interview with Mrs Thomson. She had been in tears and seemed to him to be in real distress, engaging with him in prayer. Revd McIntyre told the court he had no reason to doubt the sincerity of her grief and distress, telling the court that she was 'a good living, upright woman'.

At this point in the trial, the boy was cross-examined and reiterated his earlier statements. Addressed by His Lordship, the boy was told:

> You have admitted taking part in a very terrible act, having yourself done a very terrible act, which has had the most terrible consequences. You must understand that act might have had terrible consequences for yourself. I hope, and I am sure the jury also hope, that those who are now training you and directing and controlling you will enable you to make good the

gifts you have, and control the impulses to which your limitations may make you subject. You can go home now.

Questions were then put to the police officials by Lord Moncrieff, as to why they did not think it would have been advisable when the boy was giving his statement, to have it formally declared before a Magistrate. Further, His Lordship asked why they did not either before or after charging the boy, tell him or his father that he was entitled to the services of a solicitor. Inspector Denholm, the officer in charge of the case, replied that he thought the boy was 'well enough safeguarded by his father being there' and that his father had been satisfied with the way the boy was being treated. Lord Moncrieff then replied, 'Are you not aware that recently the opinion was expressed judicially that the police practice should be reformed and that notice of having the services of a solicitor should be given to everyone at the time of arrest?' The witness replied that he was. Lord Moncrieff then asked him, 'Now, when a person charged is prepared to make a statement, do you always consider whether it wouldn't be better that the statement should be taken before a Magistrate formally?' The witness answered that it had been a voluntary statement. This answer was challenged, however, due to the boy's mental age and the officer conceded that, with hindsight, it would have been appropriate to have had the statement taken before the Magistrate.

The trial continued and the following day Mrs Thomson again entered the witness box and was cross-examined by the Advocate Depute. Asked why she had earlier stated that she had not been surprised at her husband's death, Mrs Thomson said, 'If a drunk man goes out with a gun anything can happen'. Asked why she did not go over to the body on being told it was her husband, Mrs Thomson answered that she had been afraid. On further questioning, she also told the court that anyone could have taken the gun out of the farm kitchen without her knowledge and that she could offer no explanation of how her husband met his death. Mrs Thomson also described the boy's story as a 'complete fabrication'.

The evidence being concluded, the counsel began their addresses to the jury. The Advocate Depute told the jury that although the boy was 'a backward boy', this did not necessarily mean that his memory was not all right or that he could not give a true account of the events. He added that in the case of Mrs Thomson, 'there are circumstances in which what is known as provocation may influence a matter of this sort, and sometimes what would otherwise be murder is reduced to

The old bridge at Cambus, near Garvel Farm.
(Author's collection)

culpable homicide because an accused person has been provoked'. The Advocate
Depute continued:

Mrs Thomson may have had great provocation, but this was not
immediate provocation. This was in no sense in the heat of the
moment. It is, of course, possible to take the view – although I have
seen no indication during this case that it is to be put forward – that
Mrs Thomson's life latterly was such that her mind might have become
affected to such an extent as, while not to make her insane, to reduce her

sense of responsibility. There has been no medical evidence in support of any such case, but if it should be urged I have no strong submission to make upon that subject or upon the possibility of regarding her conduct as having been provoked, though I fail to see that such a calculated attack could have been said to have been made under provocation.

In conclusion, he asked the jury to bring in a verdict of guilty.

Mr Cameron for the defence, in his address told the jury that he was asking for 'justice at their hands on a simple issue of life and death'. He said that the tale they had been told by the prosecution was unbelievable and could not exist 'outside of a mad house'. Mr Cameron also pointed out that the axe had been found in the bothy, where the boy had resided. He also highlighted that the prosecution had offered no other evidence against Mrs Thomson other than the testimony of the boy, who was 'a self expressed liar' and 'known to be imaginative', asking the jury, 'Is there one single word in the evidence corroborating anything the boy says against Mrs Thomson? Not one.'

In summing up, Lord Moncrieff pointed out that Mr Thomson had lost his life by violence and it was clear that his wounds could not have been self-inflicted, as, 'a man who took his own life did not wound his head with five major wounds, three of which were fractures of the skull, nor did a man, having done so, resort to the double use of a shotgun'. His Lordship told the jury that the only question they had to determine was, 'by whose hand was the act performed' and whether they were satisfied that the Crown had proved that Mrs Thomson had been the one responsible. His Lordship continued, 'It is a terrible thing to trust your life to an accomplice and a more terrible thing if the accomplice is not entirely of normal responsibility.' On the question of motive, Lord Moncrieff highlighted that although Mrs Thomson had resented her husband's treatment of her, she had been seen to take lawful action against him, by complaining to the police and asking for their protection, and also contacting a solicitor in pursuit of a divorce. He pointed out that these were not the usual steps taken by a woman who, 'under the impulses of an insane hatred, was planning not only to take life' but to take life in the circumstances of which the court had heard.

The jury, after an absence of twenty-five minutes, returned with a unanimous verdict of not guilty. Mrs Thomson, who was very composed, thanked His Lordship and the jury.

Stirling Sheriff Court, where Elizabeth
Thomson was tried (Author's collection)

A large crowd had gathered outside the court in the hope of seeing Mrs Thomson, but they were disappointed as the police had taken her out by another door, where she entered a car and was taken home to Garvel Farm.

Murder of a Neighbour

The Execution of Alexander Miller, 1837

Suspect: Alexander Miller

Charge: Murder

Sentence: Execution

Alexander Miller, convicted of murder at the High Court of Justiciary, underwent the extreme penalty of the law on 8 April 1837. By two o'clock on this date, Broad Street was filled by a dense crowd, many of whom were women and children. At 2.27 p.m., Miller appeared on the platform and walked across to the drop. He was dressed in a mourning suit and carried a Bible in his hand. The executioner, who was disguised in a black wig and cloak, instantly adjusted the rope, and put on the cap, when the Revd Mr Leach commenced a short prayer. Miller, to the surprise of everyone present, suddenly kicked off his shoes with great force into the street, and then pushed up the cap from his eyes and looked around him upon the crowd. His colour was said to change to 'the indescribable hue of a livid corpse' and on the handkerchief being handed to him, he seized it instantly and threw it over the scaffold. At the same time he made a leap upwards, taking the executioner unawares, who did not respond quickly enough and Miller stood for a few seconds on the drop before it fell. It was thought that he had died immediately, having hardly moved after being thrown off. After hanging for thirty-five minutes, the body was lowered into the arms of two of his relations, and laid in a coffin, to be buried later in a passage of the jail. Hisses and groans were heard from the crowd while the body was being lowered. The *Scotsman* newspaper reported that as people were making their way home from

The hangman's noose.
(© WJB Scribe)

this execution, a serious assault was committed by 'a set of drunken blackguards', supporting the theory that even the horrific nature of these public spectacles did not deter crime.

Alexander Miller's trial had taken place a few weeks earlier, having been accused of the murder of William Jarvie, by striking him with a stick, fracturing his skull and arms. Miller had also been charged with stealing a number of articles from Jarvie. Both crimes had taken place at Jarvie's house in nearby Dennyloanhead.

Witnesses described finding the dead body of Jarvie on 12 November under a hedge near his house; his head injuries were severe and his left arm was broken. A stick had been found near the body which appeared to have grey hairs on it. The later located loot from Jarvie's house consisted of a trunk containing clothes, a watch, a bundle of old stockings and some towels. William Johnston Hoggart, a surgeon from nearby Denny, gave evidence that the stick shown in court was very likely to have caused the injuries. A colleague

A map showing Dennyloanhead and Stirling. (© The Railway Clearing House)

of Miller's told the court that Miller had been living in his house with a servant named Sally McGhee, and that he had returned home an hour after the supposed time of Jarvie's murder. Another witness, James Peatie, gave evidence that he had been in a field near the scene of the murder on the Saturday night when he saw the figure of a man about 30 yards from him, whom he thought was Miller, carrying a stick in his hand. The next witness, Mrs Brown, told the court that on the night of Jarvie's murder, Miller had come to her house 'much the worse of drink'. Although he was not making a lot of sense, she formed the opinion that he had had a quarrel with some of his friends and he had stated that there was something he had done that he could not tell them. Mrs Brown's daughter Susan, who had been present, corroborated her mother's evidence and added that when she showed Miller to the door later on, he told her that he had 'killed Willie Jarvie'. Susan also stated that Miller told her he had broken into Jarvie's house and when Jarvie came in and caught him, he committed the murder.

TRIAL OF THE DENNY MURDERER.

A newspaper clipping of a headline during the trial of Alexander Miller. (Courtesy of The Scotsman Archives)

John Campbell, a collier, told the court that Miller had come to his house on the Sunday night with Sally McGhee, and that Miller had been aware a search was being made for him. Campbell's wife stated that Sally McGhee had gone out during the night to get women's clothes in order that Miller could disguise himself. Miller had also wanted to hide in a chest in the Campbells' house, a request which was refused. On Sally's return, Miller left by the back window, dressed in women's clothes and wearing a woman's cap on his head. Miller was apprehended on the Monday by Jas Christison, the criminal officer, having been chased along the street, still dressed in his recently acquired female garments, by Christison and about forty people who had joined in the pursuit. The jury at his trial deliberated for fifty-five minutes and found Miller guilty by a majority. The trial, which had excited a great deal of interest, lasted from ten in the morning until eleven at night, a considerably long trial for this era. Alexander Miller's habits were described as being 'idle and irregular, never pursuing any steady industry, but filling up the interval in reckless dissipation'. The murder seems to have been the result of a simple disagreement between the two men arising from Miller taking his dogs through the corn field where Jarvie was working, and becoming angry when Jarvie asked him to take them away from the corn. He went to the gallows denying his crime to the end.

Lord Moncrief addressed Miller after the verdict was read, stating:

Nothing remains for us but the melancholy and very painful duty of awarding the sentence of the law for the crime of which the prisoner has been found guilty. My Lords, a great and most atrocious murder has been committed, and after a patient investigation, in which I am sure, and I think I will be borne out by your Lordships in saying, that the prisoner has had all the aid he could receive from legal ability and pains and zeal of his counsel, he has been found guilty by a Jury. It is not necessary for me to go into the details of the case, but thus much I may say, that there cannot be the smallest doubt in any man's mind that this prisoner did commit the offence. In saying this I do not mean to cast any reflection on the minority of the Jury, who, I presume, thought that the case was not fully proven; and I have no doubt they acted according to their consciences in thinking that there was a reasonable doubt of the strength of the evidence to establish the case. But on the question whether this prisoner did commit the act, I think it is not possible for any man who heard out the evidence to entertain a doubt; and I am perfectly assured that his own conscience at this time bears me witness, and the majority of the Jury witness, that he is guilty. All then, that remains for me is to propose the punishment of this Court. Murder, by the law of nature, by the law of Almighty God, and by the law of this country, can only be expiated by the life of the perpetrator. He has been found guilty of that great crime, and must suffer by the law of this country what he would suffer by that of almost every other nation, if not of all of them.

I have, therefore, nothing to propose but that the sentence to be awarded in this case must be the punishment of death, according to the established rules of this country. We are limited in the time by the act of Parliament, and in order that it may be as lengthy as the circumstances will admit and the Act allow, I propose, as the sentence, that the prisoner by executed on the 8th day of April next, within the burgh of Stirling.

Lord Medwyn then gave a speech, echoing the sentiments of the first judge:

I agree with my brother, that this is a most painful duty, but one thing is satisfactory, that we have no discretion as to the sentence to be awarded. By the verdict of the Jury – a conscientious verdict both by the majority

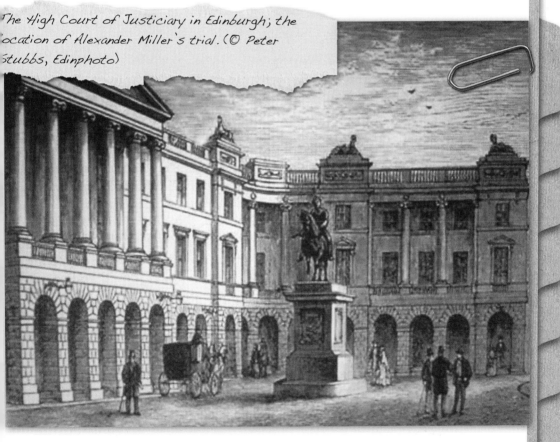

The High Court of Justiciary in Edinburgh; the location of Alexander Miller's trial. (© Peter Stubbs, Edinphoto)

and also by the minority (for I entirely concur with your Lordship in that part of your observations), the prisoner has been found guilty of a murder, a verdict which I think is consistent both with the law and justice of the case. The circumstances of this remarkable case have been too recently before us to render it necessary for me to dwell on them. I have no intention to go into the circumstances, but I may state that if affords a melancholy instance of how one may proceed from a life of offence against what may be called the smaller provisions of the criminal law, till the onward progress reaches the highest crime that man can commit. Notwithstanding the violent language he previously used against the poor old man, I do not believe he went with any mortal purpose or any fixed intention against him – I think he went only to commit the minor offence, in order to obtain the means of indulging in his unfortunate propensity. But, alas! His reasoning powers had been paralyzed, the balance of his mind had been overset, and being detected by the old man, in order to remove a dangerous witness he hesitated not to commit murder. It is somehow ordered in the Providence that directs the affairs of this world, that a murderer seldom escapes – that the blood which is shed seems to cry from the ground for vengeance; and accordingly we find, that he not only confesses his crime to the girl Brown, but almost as distinctly to the mother and other witnesses; and from conscious guilt, he went out of the back window of the house, and afterwards, in disguise, endeavoured to make his escape, pursued by the officers of justice and all the neighbours. It was then that he attempted to commit suicide, but as he said himself, God did not give him strength; and I rejoice to think he was so swayed, for while the example is beneficial, that such crimes, however silently perpetrated, should be punished openly, I may also indulge a charitable hope, that the interval may be so spent that he may appear before his Redeemer and Judge with fruits of penitence and grounds of hope, very different than if he had rushed to his everlasting doom reeking in the blood of his victim. I concur in the sentence.

Lord Meadowbank then proceeded to pass sentence, giving the following address to Miller:

Alexander Miller, you stood at that bar this morning charged with the crime of murder, and it has been proved in the course of the trial, in which I am sure your counsel has done you full justice – I say it has been proved to the satisfaction of the Court, and to the satisfaction of a majority of a Jury of your countrymen, that you are guilty of the crime of which you are charged. You stand there a most extraordinary and miserable example, an example, the like of which I have never witnessed before. You are a young man, 19 years of age, according to your own declaration, but it appears before this crime was perpetrated you had acquired a general character for recklessness – a character which led the whole countryside where you lived, when this horrible offence was known to fix on you, as the individual most likely to have committed it […] But so it is, that hurried in the moment from whatsoever view, you, young as you are, did, in a way the most barbarous, perpetrate this murder, and resisted even that plea which you yourself, when you came to reflect upon it, could not think of without being appalled – that the poor, old, and feeble object of your vengeance, should have held up his hands, imploring you not to murder him, and yet in the face of that prayer, you proceeded in the most barbarous manner to put it into execution.

But here the example does not end, for it must afford to all who have heard of your case, the powerful – the overwhelming example, of the misery that haunts a criminal, even so hardened as you are, and of the immediate effect which conscience produced upon the feelings of your own mind. From the very moment that the crime was committed you felt how deeply you had sinned both against your fellow creature, and against Almighty God. You felt the deep aggravation of your offence, and you felt what was the result of your offence if it was proved against you. And you have stated, at least it has been proved that you have stated, that it was once suggested by your paramour, that both of you should end your lives together [...] Fix your eyes on that Great Being in whose hands alone is the power of giving mercy, through the merits of your Redeemer; but let me pray and beseech you, that in that repentance you may be sincere – that in searching after the truth of the gospel, you may be sincere, and that you may listen to and profit by those instructions which I am sure will be most willingly and earnestly afforded to you. You will now attend to the sentence of the law, which it is my most heavy duty to pronounce against you.

Alexander Miller was then sentenced to be removed to Stirling Jail and undergo the punishment of death at the common place of execution in that burgh on 8 April 1837. It was reported that on being removed from the High Court of Justiciary to the nearby Calton Jail, Miller showed a callous indifference to his fate, expressing his hatred of the judge and the witnesses, and boasting of his 'swiftness of foot' which enabled him to evade capture for so long on the day he was apprehended.

Calton Jail, where Miller was taken after his trial. (© Peter Stubbs, Edinphoto)

It was well documented that Miller had no occupation, and, although stating in his declaration that he was a cooper, there was no evidence to suggest that he knew or had ever practiced this craft. It was reported that his father had also been 'a person of the same idle habits and like activity'. Miller, an excellent marksman, was known by the name of 'Scatters' due to the method in which he loaded his gun, so as to scatter the shot when it fired, enabling him to kill a quantity of game with one shot.

The Brutal Murder of Margaret Gilfillan

St Ninian's, 1894

Charge: Murder

Suspect: Daniel Gilfillan

In the Stirling village of St Ninian's on New Year's night, 1894, the brutal murder of Margaret Gilfillan took place, shocking the public by its nature. Mrs Gilfillan had been found the following afternoon, lying dead on her kitchen floor in a large pool of blood. Mrs Gilfillan had been 'cut severely about the face with a sharp instrument' and had other marks of violence over her whole body. The worst injury, however, which drew parallels with the infamous murders in the Whitechapel area of London some years earlier, was the injury to her abdominal area, which were said to have been 'lacerated to a terrible extent' and horribly mutilated.

Suspicion soon fell on Mrs Gilfillan's husband Daniel, a mill worker at Cambusbarron. Mr Gilfillan was fifty-seven years old and he and his wife had been described as 'much addicted to drinking'. Mrs Gilfillan was also described as having 'rather a loose character', which had been the cause of many quarrels between the couple, and hence it had been surmised that perhaps Mr Gilfillan had found his wife in the company of another man and had stabbed her in a moment of passion.

Gilfillan, who was well liked by those who knew him, and described as 'bearing the character of an industrious man, and when sober, was peaceable in disposition', was arrested and committed to prison for further examination.

Two pocket knives had been found on him at the time of his arrest, with the larger of the two being stained with blood on both sides of the blade. His version of events was that he and his wife had been drinking on New Year's Day, and in the evening he had gone out. On returning home at

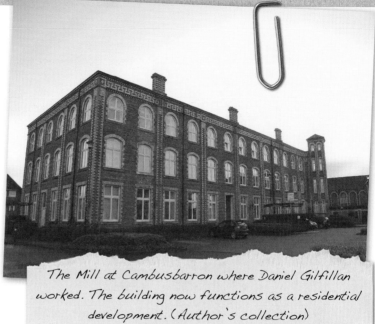

The Mill at Cambusbarron where Daniel Gilfillan worked. The building now functions as a residential development. (Author's collection)

about eight o'clock that night, he had found his wife lying drunk at the foot of the stairs leading to their house in Main Street, St Ninian's. Having dragged her upstairs, he put her on the bed and gave her some whisky. At this point, Gilfillan's grown-up son had come into the house and asked where his mother was, to which he was told by his father that she was in bed. Gilfillan and his son then went out together and attended the home of one of Gilfillan's other sons, where they enjoyed the New Year festivities, returning home at three or four o'clock in the morning. Gilfillan, who told police he had gone straight to bed, also stated that he slept until 8 a.m., when he noticed that his wife was lying in the same position he had left her in the previous evening. Gilfillan said that he asked her if she was feeling better and she told him she was. Giving her some more whisky, Gilfillan then went out and was told later in the day by a friend of his wife's that she was dead.

Mrs Gilfillan's body was taken to the mortuary at the County Buildings, and a post-mortem was carried out by Drs McFadyen and Chalmers. The post-mortem, however, did not confirm the report that her death had been caused by stabbing. It seems that, whilst at first the abdominal wounds and the excessive bleeding indicated the use of a knife or other sharp instrument, the doctors were of the opinion that the injuries may have been caused by 'a succession of brutal kicks with the toe of a heavy boot', and that no knife was used.

As Mrs Gilfillan was reportedly, 'in the habit of receiving visits from men', the case against her husband was by no means certain, particularly as Mr Gilfillan was absent from the house on New Year's day for a sufficiently long enough time to allow another person to enter the house and commit the atrocity. Having appeared in court, Gilfillan was remanded in custody and the case remitted to the Sheriff Court.

What occurred after this remains a mystery, as there is no record of there ever being a trial against Daniel Gilfillan. Indeed, he appears on the 1901 census for Stirling; therefore, it seems unlikely that he was convicted of causing his wife's death. The *Stirling Observer* reported on 10 January 1894 that a young man named Watson was sought by police for questioning, due to information from neighbours that he had been a frequent visitor to the house when Mr Gilfillan was out. However, there the trail goes cold, as there was no record of a trial for this man either and nothing further reported in the press regarding this case. It can only be assumed therefore that the charges against Daniel Gilfillan were dropped and the culprit of this atrocious crime was never caught.

Murder of a Fellow Workman

The Execution of Robert Tenant, 1833

Suspect: Robert Tenant

Charge: Murder

Sentence: Execution

Following his conviction and sentencing at the Circuit Court of Justiciary in Stirling, Robert Tennant was executed in front of the Court House in Broad Street on 2 October 1833. His crime had been the murder of William Peddie on the road near Beancross in Falkirk on 3 August 1833. The executioner drew the white cap over Tenant's head, moved him forward to the drop and put the noose around his neck. Tenant quickly dropped the handkerchief – the signal to say that he was ready. The executioner had forgotten to remove Tenant's neckcloth. It was reported that he appeared 'considerably agitated' by the delay whilst the executioner removed the neckcloth and was seen to tremble whilst he uttered, 'Oh God, oh God have mercy'. Having given the signal again, the drop fell at 8.25 a.m., with Tennant experiencing violent convulsive struggles at the end of the rope.

EXECUTION
of
Robert Tennant,

A newspaper clipping from the execution of Tenant. (Courtesy of The Scotsman Newspaper)

Tennant's victim, William Peddie, had been an old man of over seventy years, who worked alongside him. They had both been employed in breaking stones on the Carse roads. His body had been found near Beancorse, approximately 2 miles from Stirling town, and on examination it was discovered that he had several large wounds on his skull, thought to have been inflicted by a hammer, such as that used for breaking stones. A hammer which fitted this description was found not far from the body, with grey hairs and brain matter stuck to it and stained with blood. The body had been found at five o'clock in the afternoon, with a witness stating that he had seen Peddie alive and working as usual at midday, while he was passing by. Robert Tennant, a young man, was soon apprehended on suspicion of murder, as during a search of the area he had been found apparently asleep, with his feet protruding from a field of beans near the spot where the murder was committed. Tennant had denied all knowledge of the murder, stating that he had been 'the worse of liquor' and had gone into the field to sleep. Tennant was committed to Stirling Jail. It appeared that for some time, Tennant had been drinking excessively and the manager of the road had instructed that when he showed up he was to be told by Peddie, who was the foreman, that he was no longer employed there. Having drank excessively all night in nearby Grangemouth, he had gone to the toll house the following morning, where he consumed more alcohol. It was believed that after this, he had come to the road, when he took exception to being told by Peddie that the manager had ordered him to leave.

Robert Tennant was indicted for murder and stood trial at the Circuit Court of Justiciary in Stirling on 12 September 1833. At the trial, evidence was given by Henry Reid and a Mr Brock, two gentlemen who were passing along the road from Beancross at about four or five o'clock on the afternoon of 3 August. There they saw William Peddie lying on the road with a wound on the back of his head, another wound further down his head and dampness on the ground, which they realised was blood. They confirmed that Peddie had been dead, but his body was not yet stiff. The two men informed Peddie's employers what they had found. A man named David Sharp, who knew Robert Tennant, recollected that he saw him at Kerse Toll on the day in question at about three o'clock in the afternoon. Previously that day, Sharp had seen William Peddie at work breaking stones at Beancross as he passed by between eleven and twelve o'clock. Another man, Thomas Girdwood, told the court that he had seen Robert Tennant between three and four o'clock, on the road near Beancross. Tennant asked if Girdwood had seen William Peddie, and Girdwood replied that he had, having passed him about 200 and 300 yards away. The witness then went south towards Beancross and again met Peddie coming north, a little before four o'clock. Having later seen the spot where the body had been found, Girdwood confirmed that this was the spot in which he had left Tennant. The next witness, John Henry, stated that he had been on the road between Kerse Toll and Beancross, between three and four o'clock, when he saw Tennant leaning against a hedge. A little further on, he saw Peddie coming towards where Tennant had been standing. Later, John Henry had seen the body of Peddie near the place where Tennant had been. Some doubt was cast on this witness' motives for giving evidence against Tennant, however, as it had been alleged that Henry had told the woman at the toll that he would 'do for' William Peddie as he had refused to help him when his horse and cart had gotten stuck. Henry denied that he had made this statement to the woman. Another witness, John Fleming, also described seeing Tennant on the same part of the road around this time, sitting at the hedge. Witness George Shaw, who collected dung on the road near Beancross, also saw Tennant on the road, and spoke to him. When Shaw returned from the north between four and five o'clock, he again saw Tennant and Peddie talking together, and heard the name 'Borthwick' mentioned. Shaw then continued on to his house, returning later to take home the dung. At this point he saw Peddie lying lifeless at the same spot where he had seen him talking with Tennant. Shaw stated that he had only been gone from the two men for around ten minutes. He saw the wound on Peddie's head, but at first he did not see Tennant. Almost immediately, however, Tennant came out of a field of beans and asked Shaw to conceal where he had been. Shaw told him that he would not do this and, attempting to persuade him, Tennant had stated that if he concealed it, this coupled with Tennant's denial, would mean that the incident could not be proved.

Mr Borthwick, who superintended the road between Kerse Toll and Beancross, spoke of seeing Peddie at work on the day in question and confirmed that he had instructed him to dismiss Tennant, as although Peddie had previously spoken up for Tennant and tried to keep his job for him, it had become clear that Tennant's 'drinking and irregularity' had rendered him unfit to be employed any longer. Ann Smith, who kept a public house at Woodend, to the south of Beancross, saw Peddie on the day of the murder at around four o'clock, when he came to the house to ask if Tennant was there, to which she had replied that she had not seen him that day. Ann told the court that prior to the incident, the deceased and Tennant had always been on 'excellent terms'. Dr Graham, who had examined Peddie's body, gave the court a description of his wounds. He then identified two hammers which had been found near the body, one of which had Peddie's hair attached to it. Dr Graham told the court that the wounds on the deceased's head must have been inflicted by an instrument of the same nature as the ones shown. Dr Main, who had assisted in the examination, concurred with this evidence. At this point in the trial, the prisoner's declarations were read. He stated that he was twenty-four and said that he had been at Grangemouth fair, where he had gotten drunk at the toll, then went into the field of beans and fallen asleep.

Tennant denied that he had spoken to the deceased on the day in question and also denied having anything to do with the murder, further denying asking George Shaw to conceal anything regarding him. As all evidence had been heard, Mr Shaw Stewart, for the prosecution, addressed the jury, followed by

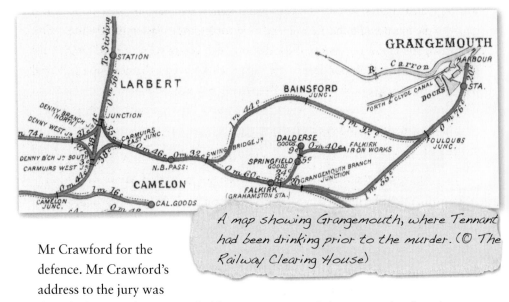

A map showing Grangemouth, where Tennant had been drinking prior to the murder. (© The Railway Clearing House)

Mr Crawford for the defence. Mr Crawford's address to the jury was described as an 'eloquent and ably argumentative defence'. Lord Gillies then summed up the evidence, expressing in the course of his observations:

> how happy he should have felt and how happy he was sure the jury would have felt, had the present painful case not fallen to their lot to determine – or were he able to discover any circumstance calculated to throw a doubt on the evidence which they had heard. If the jury credited the testimony of Shaw, the case assumed more the appearance of one of direct, than of circumstantial evidence, for he stated what was almost a confession made by the panel, of his guilt.

After his Lordship had read his notes of the evidence, the jury retired and, after an absence of about thirty minutes, returned to court and delivered their verdict, unanimously finding Robert Tennant guilty of murder, but recommending leniency on account of his previous good character and the fact that there appeared to be no premeditation or malice on his part against the deceased. On hearing this, Lord Gillies told the jury that if there were no previous malice, then there was no murder. Mr Crawford immediately moved for an arrest of judgement, on the grounds that the verdict as returned was not one of guilty of murder, but of culpable homicide. The jury then retired to reconsider the terms of the verdict, and on their return to court, Mr Crawford objected to a second verdict being received. His objection, however, was overruled and the verdict allowed. The second verdict detailed that Tennant was guilty of the murder and the recommendation for leniency was on the grounds of his previous good character, and that the murder had in fact been premeditated. Lord Gillies proceeded to pronounce sentence, giving what was described as 'an earnest and feeling address' to the prisoner. Robert Tennant was sentenced to be:

> [...] carried back to the Tolbooth of Stirling, and to be there maintained on bread and water till Wednesday 2 October, and on that day, between the hours of eight and ten in the morning, to be taken to the place of execution at Stirling, and be there hanged by the neck on a gibbet till he be dead, and that his body be afterwards interred within the precincts of Stirling Jail.

Tennant was said to have displayed 'little or no emotion' at the judgement.

Following the trial, in the lead up to his execution, Tennant admitted that he had killed William Peddie, but added that although he struck him, he did not intend to kill him.

Following the execution, as the executioner was proceeding through Castlehill on his way back to Edinburgh, a crowd followed him until he reached some gardens near the bridge. The executioner took shelter in one of the gardens to try and evade the mob; however, they found him there and proceeded to attack him. The executioner ran towards the river, but was followed by the crowd, who threw stones after him. He finally got to safety when he plunged into the river and swam to the opposite side, by which time the high constables had arrived, successfully managing to drive off the crowd. The man was taken to the jail for safety and two men were taken into custody, charged with assault.

SOLVED

Grave Robbing

The Notorious James McNab, 1823

Suspect: James McNab
Charge: Grave Robbing

The grave of Mary Witherspoon in the Old Town Cemetery in Stirling. (Author's collection)

On 5 April 1823, it was reported that John Forrest, James McNab and Daniel Mitchell had been indicted to stand trial at the Stirling Circuit Court, charged with 'violating the sepulchres of the dead'. Their crime had been opening up the grave of Mary Witherspoon, a woman of fifty-five years of age who had been buried on 19 November 1822, having died from dropsy a few days earlier. James McNab was the town's gravedigger at this time, and, as such, had knowledge of the freshest corpses that could be stolen to give to medical students willing to pay for the bodies to use them for dissection. Helped by Daniel Mitchell, McNab had gone to the grave of Mary Witherspoon a few evenings after her funeral to steal the body. However, the pair did not manage to evade the law for long and were soon caught.

It was established that John Forrest, an

Grave Robbing

Edinburgh medical student, had been the intended recipient for the body – therefore he was also named on the indictment. Before the Anatomy Act of 1832, the only bodies that were available for dissection were of those condemned to death by the courts, however, with the growth of medical teaching in Edinburgh and Glasgow, there were simply not enough bodies to go around. Therefore, the dreadful deed of grave robbing became a popular practice, particularly as some unscrupulous doctors were willing to pay well for fresh corpses.

The precognition against the men, now held in the National Archives of Scotland, stated that their actions had been to:

> [...] proceed to the churchyard or burying ground, and did then wickedly and feloniously raise and take out of the ground the dead body of the said Mary Stevenson, or Witherspoon, and did carry away the same towards Edinburgh in a chaise or otherwise.

It appeared that Forrest had approached McNab on a number of occasions – knowing McNab to be the gravedigger and having access to the keys of the churchyard – in order to try and persuade him to help in removing the bodies of those recently buried. Having been identified as the 'chief aggressor', Forrest had, unfortunately for the authorities, left the country, and therefore the trial could not go ahead. As this meant the evidence against the other two was incomplete, the charge against them was deserted *pro loco et tempore*, giving the authorities the option to bring a fresh indictment against them at a later date, and they were remanded back to prison. As no new warrant was granted against them, however, they were permitted to leave the jail at around seven o'clock that evening.

Provost Thomson, aware of the strong public feeling against these men, had concerns that their release could induce a riot in the town. Having communicated these concerns to the appropriate persons, the Advocate Depute drew up a petition to the judge for a fresh warrant for their committal. Unfortunately this was not done in time, as although the two men had been liberated and managed to reach their respective homes, they had been observed leaving the jail and in a short time word had spread among the community and a crowd consisting initially of mainly women and boys, soon made their way to the home of James McNab. Having failed to break his door open with a large stone, they turned their attention to the window, shattering it to pieces. With stones raining through the open window, McNab, who was sitting by the fire, was hit on the head. Luckily for McNab, however, the police arrived and put a stop to the disturbance, taking him to the jail for safety. The undeterred crowd, now joined by many of the men of the town, then made their way to the

A view of St John Street in 2011. (Author's collection)

home of Daniel Mitchell in St John Street, where they managed to get hold of him, despite the efforts of the police.

Mitchell was knocked down, kicked and beaten, and it was reported that the clothes were torn from his back in the attack before he managed to get to a nearby house and lock the door. This did not stop the mob, however, who rushed at the door and demolished the windows, gaining entrance to the house. Mitchell, by this point, had escaped out of a door at the back of the house and made his way to a house in the same close. The Sheriff, accompanied by Provost Thomson, then arrived on the scene with Captain Jeffrey of the 77th Regiment. The Sheriff and Provost got into the middle of the mob and managed to reason with them just in time – as they had by this point gotten hold of Mitchell again – and persuaded the crowd to give him over to the authorities in order that he could be lodged in prison. Many of the mob moved aside at this point, with the exception of a few men who were shouting that they would 'take the heart out of him and tear him to pieces'. Finding that reasoning with this faction was hopeless, the Provost and Sheriff sent to the castle for a party of the 77th Regiment. On their arrival, Mitchell was taken into custody, but in the confusion that arose, blows were exchanged and some shots were fired, with the soldiers having to present their bayonets to the people to keep them at bay. The Crown responded by raining stones on to the soldiers, several of whom were knocked down. When Mitchell was finally lodged in the jail, the situation eventually calmed down.

Unfortunately though, there is no further record of these two men ever standing trial for this crime. It can only be assumed that without John Forrest, the case against them could not go ahead.

John Forrest, due to his non appearance at court, had the sentence of 'outlawry' passed against him. This meant that he would be 'outside the protection of the law' and would be stripped of all his civil rights. However, it seems that he was subsequently pardoned by the King and went on to enjoy a long career in the medical profession. It was often the case that no charges would be brought against the doctor who had instigated or turned a blind eye to the theft of corpses from graveyards.

SOLVED

Reckless Driving in St Ninian's

A Defence of Temporary Insanity, 1925

Suspect:	Thomas Ritchie
Age:	31
Charge:	Reckless Driving

At a sitting of the High Court of Justiciary in Stirling, thirty-one-year-old Thomas Ritchie found himself on trial for knocking down and killing Hugh Welsh, a local tailor and football club official, in Main Street, St Ninian's on 20 October 1925. Ritchie, described as a 'young man of fine physique', was accused of having 'driven a motor car in a culpable and reckless manner, and at an excessive speed, failed to keep a proper look out and to pay sufficient attention to the safe driving thereof', to which he pleaded not guilty.

A special defence was entered on behalf of Ritchie, that he was unaware of the presence of Hugh Welsh on the road

A 1920s car. (© Lars-Göran Lindgren)

Reckless Driving ...

due to 'the incidence of temporary mental dissociation, due to toxic exhaustive factors'. This was also the reason given for Ritchie's failure to stop, as it was alleged he was 'incapable of appreciating his own immediately previous and subsequent actings'. The jury in this case had a fairly difficult task ahead as this was a fairly unique case for the time, with motor cars being a relatively new invention, coupled with the added defence of temporary insanity.

The first witness, sixty-year-old blacksmith James Wright, told the court that he and his friend Hugh Welsh had attended a municipal ward meeting and afterwards were standing in Main Street, St Ninian's when he saw something 'flash past' and simultaneously felt a sharp stinging pain in his leg. This was followed by the sound of glass smashing, at which point Wright realised that a motor car had hit something. Looking round he saw his friend lying 'half a dozen yards away', and realised that he had been seriously injured. Having shouted for help, several people came quickly and joined Wright to try and help. The car's speed had been so great that Wright had not seen it approach.

The next witness, twenty-five-year-old James Thomson, told the court that he was standing at the nail works' corner when he saw a car approaching from the direction of Stirling town. Thomson said the car had been going 'at an excessive speed' and remarked at the time that the car would not be able to 'take the corner'. A moment later he saw the car, and, instead of turning into Borestone Crescent, it

The corner of Weaver Row and Main Street, looking towards Borestone Crescent. (Author's collection)

kept going down Main Street, at which point a loud crash was heard. Thomson told the court that he then saw the body of a man rolling behind the car, with the car making a slight movement to the right then continuing straight on. Having gone over to the man, whom he recognised as Hugh Welsh, Thomson could see that he was 'past all aid'. Continuing on to the police station, Thomson told the police there what had happened.

Other witnesses gave similar evidence, all commenting on the speed at which the car was travelling. It is interesting to note what was considered an excessive speed at this time, as most witnessed estimated the speed of the car to be between 30 and 45 miles an hour. In 1925, this was a fast speed for a car to be travelling, as cars then could not reach anywhere near the speeds we are used to today. Additionally, people were not used to cars at this time and so were not as road smart as people should be today, therefore a car travelling at 45 miles per hour, which was probably not too far from its top speed, would certainly have caused a commotion, particularly as the speed limit was 20 miles per hour at this time.

Evidence was then given by forensic expert Professor Glaister of Glasgow University. The Professor told the court that the cause of death was extensive fractures of the skull, produced by 'extreme violence such as was encountered in motor car injuries'. Other witnesses spoke of seeing Welsh bleeding extensively from his nose, mouth and ears just after the impact.

Twenty-four-year-old Eva Murch, a restaurant manageress who had known the accused for several years, told the court that on the night in question they had gone for a run in Ritchie's car, passing through Bridge of Allan and Dunblane on the way to Gleneagles. On returning to Stirling they had gone to a restaurant, leaving at ten o'clock at night, at which point Ritchie had dropped her off before leaving to return to Glasgow. Eva Murch also told the court that Ritchie's actions had not been in any way out of the ordinary that evening, despite having had a glass of sherry in the restaurant. She did, however, point out that she knew he had been in hospital for three months, during which time he had undergone a serious operation and he had recently told her that he was having trouble sleeping at night.

Several police witnesses were then called, who spoke of the movements of the car in Stirling prior to the occurrence and of the subsequent car chase which had taken place. One of the constables told the court that when they caught up with the car about a mile out of Doune, Ritchie had smelt strongly of drink but did not appear to be drunk. At this time, not being drunk was the only real requirement, as it was to be another forty years before drink drive limits were established.

Inspector Young of the Stirling Burgh Police stated that when Ritchie was brought to the police office, he said that he had been going through St Ninian's and had felt a bump, but did not realise what had happened. Inside the car, the Inspector found a man's bonnet which Ritchie said did not belong to him, and glass from the smashed windscreen.

Dr Penman, the Burgh Medical Officer of Health for Stirling, had been called to examine Ritchie during the night, in order to establish whether he had been driving whilst drunk. Having conducted some simple tests on Ritchie – getting him to do some arithmetic and walk in a straight line – Dr Penman unsurprisingly determined that he was sober, as, after all, it had been a few hours since the accident at this point.

At the second day of the trial, evidence was heard by expert in mental diseases, Dr Ivan McKenzie, who had examined Ritchie and produced a report of his findings, with reference to the defence put forward in the case. Dr McKenzie had found that Ritchie had a 'definite recollection' of leaving Stirling that night and had known that he had not travelled far on the road when he felt his car 'bump'. Ritchie had told Dr McKenzie that he thought at the time that the bump was due to the springs on the car, although his mind was 'hazy' at the time. He had also said that the first recollection of what had happened occurred to him near Doune, feeling at that point that his orientation had returned to normal. Ritchie's general health was then explored, with the court being told about his injuries suffered during the First World War. Having enlisted in September 1914, Ritchie had sustained wounds in the chest and back, with what was described as 'a gathering' in his right lung, leading to his discharge in early 1917. This old injury seemed to cause further problems in 1925, when Ritchie was admitted to Bellahouston Hospital with pain in his shoulder. At this time an opening was made in his chest, and a tube was inserted to drain the fluid. In all other respects, however, including mentally, Ritchie seems to have been healthy, and was described as 'above the average in physique and intelligence'. Dr McKenzie's opinion, based on his assessment of Ritchie, was that his recollection of the accident was impaired, although 'not in the nature of a complete loss of memory', and that this was a 'well-known phenomena' in cases of 'nervous instability' following an accident. Dr McKenzie did, however, stress that 'there was nothing in [Ritchie's] history or present state to indicate that he was suffering from toxic exhaustive factors', which were thought to be poisons caused by disease. In the doctor's opinion, Ritchie's actions following the accident were due to shock.

Evidence for the defence was then presented to the court, with Ritchie's employer, Timothy Warren, describing him as a 'reliable, capable and conscientious' manager of the ironworks. A Colonel from Ritchie's former regiment also spoke of Ritchie's character, describing him as 'a most trustworthy and reliable young man', who could not be associated with any 'cowardly action'. Another doctor from the Bellahouston Hospital gave evidence which conflicted with Dr McKenzie's, describing Ritchie as having been in a 'very serious condition owing to the absorption of toxins from his wounds' after his operation in 1925.

The next person to give evidence was Ritchie himself. He told the court that he had arrived in Stirling at 6.15 p.m. on the day in question, and had gone to the Golden Lion Hotel, where he had a whisky and soda. Ritchie said that he had no other alcoholic drink that evening other that the glass of sherry at supper. He told the court that on proceeding home that night, he had no recollection of seeing a policeman signalling to him, but he did remember hearing the sound of a whistle, which at the time he didn't think was directed at him. Ritchie said that some distance further on he had felt a jolt, but had came to the conclusion that the springs on the car had gone wrong. Having remembered passing some houses, the next thing he remembered was coming to a sudden stop at the side of a hedge. Ritchie told the court that if he had known at the time that he had seriously injured a man, he would have come to a standstill. Continuing with his evidence, he said that he had no recollection of seeing the crowd at the corner of Main Street, or of passing through Stirling. Ritchie maintained that he had no idea how he had come to be in Doune, and said he had been 'thunderstruck' when the police charged him with killing a man. He told the court that he now understood that his 'psychological condition might be such as to be attended by special danger in the event of his driving a car' and it was his intention 'never again to drive a car unless with the full authority of competent and skilled medical advisers'.

Defence witness Dr Henderson of Glasgow, a specialist in mental diseases, was then questioned regarding toxic effects from disease. Dr Henderson stated that 'toxins which had a bad effect on the body would also be likely to have an effect on the mind' and that 'a man whose war wounds were still troubling him

was a man who was liable to severe nervous disturbance'. Dr Henderson went on to say that although Ritchie himself was not in a position to realise it, on the day of the accident he had not been in a fit state to undertake such an 'exhaustive journey'.

The final witness for the defence, Dr Adams, also of Glasgow, expressed the view that this was a case of 'dissociation', and the driving of the car had been done by 'automatic action'.

As the trial went into its third day, Mr Maitland for the

THE ST NINIANS TRAGEDY.

A newspaper clipping of a headline around the time of Ritchie's murder trial. (Courtesy of The Scotsman Archives)

Crown addressed the jury with a speech that seemed to do little but help the defence, saying that:

The driving of a motor car was an act which had to be attended with respect, for a motor car was a dangerous weapon, and no man had a right to drive a car unless he was satisfied that he was in a fit state to do so, and to take proper care for the safety of other persons. In this case it was not maintained by the defence that the way the accused drove the car was anything but reckless and culpable. He submitted that it was proved beyond a doubt that the car was driven in a culpable and reckless manner, and that it was the accused who was the driver. With regard to the second matter, the defence was unique in the law of Scotland. Such a defence had never been put forward before, but none the less it was worthy – perhaps all the more worthy – of the jury's careful consideration. It was that the accused, by reason of the incidence of temporary mental dissociation, due to toxic exhaustive factors, was unaware of the presence of the deceased upon the highway and of his injury and death, and was incapable of appreciating his own immediately previous and subsequent actions. It was not a plea of insanity, it was a plea something less than that, and the jury would have to consider that state of mind carefully. To justify any verdict but one of guilty they would have to hold that owing to the accused's state of mind at the time he was totally irresponsible for his actions, but that did not end the mater, because it was open to them to consider whether, though not entirely irresponsible for his actions, he was, nevertheless, owing to the state of his health, only partially responsible for what he was doing. In that case, the appropriate verdict was guilty with a recommendation to mercy. Disassociation, meant that the man was not himself, that in some way, normal consciousness had been switched off to some other consciousness. This was a special defence, and it was for the defence to prove it. With regard to the question of dissociation no satisfactory evidence had been submitted, and as regards toxic exhaustion the doctors varied. The Crown case was that the man was perfectly normal until he had driven the lady home, and that where an abnormal state of mind was found it came on gradually. The defence said that in a moment the man ceased to be himself. The true case was that when he did this he did drive too fast and allowed his mind to wander. The interest of the day was done, and, in coming to this dangerous corner before he expected, he suddenly saw this man and knocked him down. That was the actual explanation of the accident, and was admitted by the doctors. Undoubtedly, after striking the man there were abnormalities in the accused's conduct, but he did not suggest for a minute that after knocking the man down he deliberately went on. His suggestion was that when he did strike the man, as every decent man would, he received a very severe shock, and shock, it had been admitted, could and did on occasion cause partial clouding of the memory alike of the events of the time and before and after; and shock explained and was quite in accordance with the medical theory and medical knowledge, all the accused's actions after striking the man.

Mr Maitland then went on to suggest that the correct verdict in this case was one of guilty, with a recommendation for leniency.

Mr Moncrief, for the defence, then took his turn in addressing the jury, stating:

In this case there had been the taking of a life, and it was the grave and solemn duty of the jury to hold the balance of justice in a matter that might fix the indelible stain of crime upon the man who stood before them in innocence and honour. It was as old as history that as a consequence of traffic on the roads accidents must happen. Misadventure was one of the accidents of life incurring no measure of responsibility, and in this case the events of 20 October fell into this chapter – that it was the result of a blind force directed by an involuntary factor which operated in the taking of this life, and that accordingly or inevitably the verdict on the indictment must be one of not guilty. On the cardinal facts there was really no dispute. The prosecution agreed that there was some interference to this man's normal mental condition, and if there was it was acting prior to the accident – that in short, dissociation was at work.

In summing up, Lord Murray considered that the whole question was that of when the abnormal influences began, whether they were prior to the accident or due to the accident, and that it was upon this that the question of culpability depended.

The jury, returning after an absence of five minutes, returned a unanimous verdict of not guilty, due to the accused 'suffering from abnormality at the time and therefore not culpable'.

Assault and Robbery

The Execution of Alexander O'Kane, 1812

Suspect: Alexander O'Kane
Charge: Assault and Robbery
Sentence: Execution

Alexander O'Kane faced the last sentence of the law on 21 February 1812 for the assault and robbery of cattle dealer, Archibald Stewart. Whilst awaiting his sentence, O'Kane was occasionally visited by the clergymen of Stirling, and on this fateful day, he was accompanied to the place of execution at Broad Street by Catholic priest, Mr McDonald, and another clergyman, Mr Henry. As the time of the execution approached, the priest read prayers in the council room and Mr Henry prayed, along with O'Kane. On his appearance on the scaffold, O'Kane appeared very penitent, again kneeling and praying. At about three o'clock, he dropped the handkerchief to signal that he was ready and fell from the scaffold, dying instantly. The scene was witnessed by a crowd of around 4,000 spectators.

O'Kane's crime had been attacking Archibald Stewart, a cattle dealer who had just arrived in Stirling from Falkirk, where he had received a large sum of money through his business transactions. The incident occurred on 11 October, which, coincidentally, had been the same day an execution was taking place in Stirling. O'Kane was said to have struck Stewart on the head, wounding him severely and rendering him unconscious, and stole the sum of £1,010 from him. At the start of O'Kane's trial at the High Court of Justiciary in Edinburgh, it was found that Stewart did not have a firm grasp of the English language, being a speaker of Gaelic. Therefore, a Gaelic-speaking gentleman, who happened to be in court, was sworn in to act as an interpreter. Stewart told the court through the interpreter that he had arrived in Stirling around dusk on the day in question with the money from his earnings in his possession, and found a place to lodge at Henry Abercrombie's house in Mary's Wynd (now St Mary's Wynd). At this time, St Mary's Wynd suffered from overcrowding and had some of the worst living conditions in the town. The Wynd itself was said to have been only 14ft wide and entry to the houses was by dark narrow closes.

St Mary's Wynd. (Author's collection)

Stewart dined at Abercrombie's house in the evening and afterwards went out by himself to have a drink. On returning to Abercrombie's house, at an entry way at the end of the house he saw two or three men coming towards him and he received a blow on the head which stunned him. One of the men then took the money from him and left him in the entry way, where he eventually managed to get up and get inside the house, badly cut and bruised from his ordeal.

Once Stewart was inside the house, a surgeon was sent for. It took Stewart several days to recover from his injuries. Unfortunately, as it was dark at the time of the attack (street lighting being several years away at this point), and, as he had been stunned by the blow to his head, he was unable to give a description of the men. Witnesses at the trial, however, spoke of seeing O'Kane at Falkirk Tryst on the 9th and 10th October, where Stewart was conducting business, and thinking that he looked like a 'suspicious character'. Falkirk Tryst was the site of a large cattle market at this time. The cattle markets there were busy and bustling, with buyers coming from all over Britain, and cattle, sheep and horses displayed in their thousands.

Other witnesses spoke of seeing O'Kane in Stirling on 11 October, which was the day of the attack on Stewart, and also of seeing him in the vicinity around the time the assault occurred. A cooper in the town, Charles Monteith, whose shop was next door to where Stewart had lodged, told the court that he had seen O'Kane on 11 October in Mary's Wynd with a boy. O'Kane had seemed inclined to go up one of the lanes, but the boy did not appear willing, and Mr Monteith then saw them move on, walking with a woman 'of no good appearance', whom he knew to be Mary McNair, the wife of one of the men executed in Stirling that day for theft. Other witnesses spoke of seeing O'Kane and the boy in various public houses in other towns following the date of the incident, and noticing that they appeared to have a large sum of money in their possession. Eventually ending up in Dumfries, O'Kane stayed at an inn, sleeping in a back room over the kitchen. As suspicion had been aroused by O'Kane's extravagance throughout the nearby towns, he was apprehended and found to have bank notes in the waistband of his trousers. On searching his room at the inn, a parcel containing bank notes was found concealed in the chimney. O'Kane, who had originally denied being in Stirling on the day of the assault, later changed his mind and admitted that he had been there and had witnessed a fight, after which he found bank notes lying on the ground. After hearing all the evidence presented, the jury returned a verdict of guilty, and O'Kane was accordingly sentenced to be hanged.

A Selection of Stirling Court Cases from the Circuit Court of Justiciary

The Function of the Circuit Court of Justiciary

As the only High Court of Justiciary for Scotland was in Edinburgh, the Circuit Court would come to other cities routinely to hear the more serious cases, typically assault, fraud, culpable homicide or murder. High Court trials were held before a judge and jury, and could give very lengthy prison sentences and in the Georgian and Victorian eras, could also give the sentence of death by hanging. The Circuit Court of 1834 saw some unusual cases – among them was the case of Burnet Quigley and Charles Cameron who were both accused of having stolen a 'lock-fast' box containing an assortment of cutlery, from a house in Stirling. Cameron, who was out on bail, had failed to appear and was thereby outlawed. Quigley, who pleaded guilty, was sentenced to six months' imprisonment.

Another case at the same sitting of the Circuit Court was that of James Kier, who had been accused of assaulting William Brown, a farmer from Glenside. The charge detailed that Kier had struck Brown 'several severe blows on the head' with a hammer 'to the effusion of his blood'. Kier pleaded not guilty and the case went to trial after a jury had been assembled. After the evidence had been heard, the jury – without retiring to consider their verdict – found him guilty. Kier was sentenced to twelve months' imprisonment.

An alternative to imprisonment and the death sentence was that of 'transportation', sometimes called 'penal transportation'. This popular court disposal was the deporting of convicted criminals to the colonies either for life or for a set period of time. On arriving at their destination, convicts were expected to carry out unpaid physical work. Female convicts often worked as domestic servants. Once a convict had served part of their time, they could apply for a 'ticket of leave', which would give them some freedoms and allow them to live a more normal life in the colonies. Transportation, which was usually the result of a High Court trial, was seen as the humane alternative to execution, however, as we will see, this sentence was often given for fairly petty offences. The sentencing of people to transportation ended in the late 1860s, but was still in place in 1833, however, when stealing a coat from a house in Melville Place, Stirling, landed James Smith in court. As Smith had been previously convicted of theft, the court decided a sentence of 'transportation for life' was appropriate.

In the same year, 'transportation for life' was also the fate of Alexander Stewart, a porter from Stirling who was accused of having 'written and fabricated' a letter to Robert Gillies and of 'having fraudulently used and uttered it as genuine', to receive a payment of £10 in poor relief. Some years later, Robert Bennet was found guilty of having stolen a watch from a house in Cambusbarron, and was sentenced to the lesser punishment of seven years' transportation.

The sentence of transportation appeared not to function terribly well as a deterrent, however, as shown by the case of Helen Armstrong in 1855. Having previously served a sentence of seven years' transportation, Armstrong had returned to Stirling on a ticket of leave. Before long, however, Armstrong had been charged with stealing some iron goods from a house in King Street and also two shirts from a house in St Mary's Wynd. Keeping herself busy, Armstrong had then gone into the home of John Pollock, a publican, stealing 3½ yards of cotton cloth, followed by the theft of several other articles from a drying green at Albert Place. Clearly not amused by these activities, the court sentenced Armstrong to a further fifteen years' transportation.

A convict ship, typical of that used for penal transportation. (Author's collection)

Theft

Cases of theft were frequently seen in the courts, with one notable case: 'The Great Theft of Jewellery by a Clerk at Stirling Station', which appeared before a judge in 1854. William Jenkins, a young man, was charged with having stolen a parcel bearing the address: Mrs Burnet, 240 Gallowgate, Glasgow; and a silver watch belonging to James Pinkerton, a gamekeeper at Mansion House Place, London, whilst he was employed as a clerk at Stirling railway station. Jenkins was also charged with having stolen several items from a carpet bag, which he was said to have forced open; and some jewellery and other items from a chest, which belonged to Ann Smith from Manchester. Jenkins pleaded guilty and evidence was given to the court of his previous good character, which Lord Wood took into account, stating, 'It is exceedingly melancholy to see a boy of your age, and one in regard to whom testimony has been borne that until now he has sustained an excellent character, placed at the bar of this court on such a charge as that to which you have pleaded guilty'. However, Lord Wood, explaining that the crime was one of 'a very aggravated nature', went on to say, 'I am, therefore, under the necessity of inflicting a punishment which I hope will have the effect not only of preventing you in future from committing such an act, but will also effectually deter others from such conduct who are placed in such circumstances as you were'. Jenkins was then sentenced to penal servitude for four years.

The following year, the theft of several items from a grocer's shop in Port Street, along with the sum of £10, was the charge faced by James Ross. Pleading not guilty, a jury were assembled and Ross underwent a trial. After testimony from several witnesses, Ross was found guilty and sentenced to six years' penal servitude.

Another case of railway station theft was dealt with by the Circuit Court in 1872. John Waywell and William McKay faced trial for stealing trinkets and American bonds

Stirling railway station in the nineteenth century. (Author's collection)

from a portmanteau on the platform of Stirling station. Waywell, who had one previous conviction, was sentenced to fifteen months' imprisonment, while McKay, who had three previous convictions, was sentenced to seven years' penal servitude.

Alexander Jack, another employee at the Caledonian railway station in Stirling also fell foul of the law in 1875, charged with the theft of tartan cloth, tweed cloth, ladies' and mens' gloves and ladies' bonnets. The thefts took place over the course of nearly a year before Jack was caught, with some of the articles being found in his house in Spittal Street. Jack, a night watchman at the station, had intended to 'reset' the articles, meaning to sell them on for money. Pleading guilty, he was sentenced to eighteen months' imprisonment, which was a more lenient sentence than he would have received due to the local minister and a number of Stirling merchants speaking on his behalf to his usual good character.

In 1886, James Steel, described as 'an intelligent-looking man', pleaded not guilty to a charge of breaking into a house in Glasgow Road, St Ninian's and stealing a large quantity of silverware. The evidence given detailed that Steel had been observed near the house around the time of the break-in, carrying his shoes in his hand and a small parcel under his arm. He was seen later in the morning in the wood on Coxithill Farm, and the next day he was apprehended coming out of the wood with the parcel of silver articles under his arm. Steel, who had conducted his own defence and had objected to being photographed against his will by the Stirling police, told the court that he had simply 'found' the parcel in the woods. The jury, without needing to retire to consider their verdict, found him guilty as libelled. Steel was then addressed by Lord Young, who said:

I have very much distress in dealing with your case. You seem to have gone early astray. In 1860 you were convicted of theft, and had sentence of 12 months imprisonment passed upon you by the Sheriff at Perth. In 1862 you were again convicted before the Sheriff at Perth and had sentence of 12 calendar months imprisonment; and in 1870 you were again convicted before the same Sheriff and sentenced to 3 months imprisonment. Then you were convicted of robbery before the Circuit Court of Justiciary at Perth in 1870, and sentenced to penal servitude for seven years; and, lastly, you were convicted before myself, sitting in the Circuit Court of Perth, and sentenced to ten years penal servitude and five years' police supervision. You say that you are only 34 years of age – the police in Perth say you are over 40 – but your case is a hopeless one. The way of transgressors is certainly hard. A man who has gone astray as you have done cannot get to the right road again. The condition of society is so strong against it that it requires a man of very much more resolution and energy than you appear to be to have any prospect of getting back; and really the only question seems to be how society is to be protected against you as a common pest. I had occasion to say today already that at a time not so remote you would simply have been put out of the way as a noxious animal. You would have been hanged as a person unfit to live. You cannot reform; you are one of the breakages of humanity, and it is really with sincere pain that I contemplate what it is my duty to do with you. I have seen prisoner after prisoner in your position sentenced to penal servitude for life, in my younger days, for much less – prisoners who proved incorrigible, and the protection of society required that they should be shut up. I cannot bring my mind to do that today; but I will make a cessation of your evil-doing for as long a period as I did upon the last occasion. It may be my duty to make the sentence much more severe, but I simply sentence you again to penal servitude for ten years and police supervision for five years.

Expert Witnesses and the Crime of Culpable Homicide

During the Georgian and Victorian eras, there was a growing importance in Medical Jurisprudence, the branch of study which connected medicine and law. The first Professorship of Forensic Medicine to be established in a British university occurred in Edinburgh in 1801, and during the nineteenth century there were many advances in the discovery of physiological action of drugs and poisons, and in anatomy, physiology and microscopy. Often, in the more complex cases involving murder or culpable homicide, expert witsesses could be called to give evidence. These men were often called upon to perform post-mortems when a death was thought to be caused by a criminal act. Forensic medicine was very much in its infancy and science was not widely used in criminal investigations, however, more and more emphasis was being placed on medical evidence in trials. Post-mortems at his time provided very useful information for criminal trials, although the manual, *Practical Pathology for Students and Practitioners*, published in 1892, while providing in-depth instructions on carrying out post-mortems, also showed how rudimentary these procedures could be, by giving instructions on how to prepare the area if the post-mortem was to be carried out in a private house:

> A good firm kitchen table is to be placed in the room where the cadaver is lying. (If this cannot be obtained, the coffin lid, or a door removed from its hinges and supported by a couple of chairs, is a good substitute.) The room should be well lighted, and as large and airy as possible; where it is small the windows should be thrown wide-open…Clean rags, a number of newspapers, three or four sponges, a piece of soap and several towels, are essential. The hands of the operator are first thoroughly washed with warm water and turpentine; a stream of cold water is then allowed to run over them; after which they should be thoroughly anointed with the carbolic oil; or if this is not at hand, with olive oil lard, or with one of the above mixtures. The palms of the hands should then be carefully wiped with a clean, dry cloth, in order to allow of a firm grip of knives, or other instruments, being taken. From time to time during the section the stream of cold water should again be run over the hands, or they should be dipped and rubbed in a bowl of cold water placed between the legs of the subject.

Due to the serious implications of finding a person guilty of murder, a charge which had originally began as one of murder would often be reduced to culpable homicide, for which there was no death penalty. The crime of culpable homicide, therefore, was often seen before the courts. In 1875, the Circuit Court dealt with one such case, involving the death of a molecatcher named John Nicholson, who was said to have been assaulted by Daniel and Margaret McCoull and thrown over a parapet wall into St John Street. Both accused, who had been remanded in prison at Stirling, pleaded not guilty to the charges. At the trial, the first witness called was Ann Pope from St Mary's Wynd, whose mother had a lodging house where Daniel and Margaret McCoull had come to stay a few weeks before the incident.

Miss Pope told the court that the pair had both been drunk on the day in question and John Nicholson had come into the house stating that Margaret McCoull had thrown a stone at him. A quarrel then began between the two accused and John Nicholson outside in the courtyard. Miss Pope went on to say that when she went outside, she saw Daniel McCoull strike Nicholson, and while the three of them were on the parapet wall, she saw Daniel McCoull holding Nicholson by the legs with his body hanging over the wall. Margaret McCoull was then seen to strike Nicholson twice on the face and heard to shout to her husband to throw Nicholson over the wall, which he did. Miss Pope said that she then went inside the house, thinking that nothing serious had happened as the height of the drop on the other side of the wall was only a few feet. She told the court that both Daniel and Margaret McCoull were both quiet people when sober, but violent when drunk.

Other witnesses, neighbours of Miss Pope, gave corroborative evidence. Henry Reid, who had been with John Nicholson that day told the court that they had been drinking and that he had called Margaret McCoull offensive names, which led to someone throwing a stone at him, which had hit Nicholson instead. Evidence was then given by Dr William Forrest, who had conducted the post-mortem along with his son, Dr James Forrest. He explained that death had been caused by the effusion of blood on the brain as a result of a bruise on the head caused by the fall. The jury, taking only five minutes to consider the verdict, returned with a unanimous verdict of guilty. Daniel McCoull was sentenced to nine months' imprisonment and Margaret McCoull to twelve months' imprisonment.

Culpable homicide was also the charge faced by Alexander McCulloch in 1846, after being accused of 'recklessly and culpably failing to attend properly to two laden carts, each drawn by one horse, of which he was in charge' on the road between Stirling and Alloa. The result of McCulloch's lack of care had been that an infant child who had strayed before one of the carts, was trampled down and killed by the wheels passing over him. McCulloch pleaded guilty and was sentenced to three months' imprisonment.

Another case was heard in the Circuit Court in 1863. Charles Buchan, employed as a shop boy to John Chalmers, a Stirling druggist, was charged with culpable homicide and 'culpable neglect of duty'. John McAllister, who lived in Baker Street,

A typical nineteenth-century druggist shop. (Author's collection)

had gone into the Dduggist shop asking for some cough medicine for his two-year-old son. Buchan accordingly handed over a cough mixture containing morphia and opium, with instructions of the dose to be administered.

When the child died from taking the mixture, Buchan was charged due to the fact that he had not asked the age of the child or the nature of the illness for which the medicine was intended.

In court, Buchan's advocate argued that it was not the duty of the accused to make these enquiries, and that he had merely supplied the mixture which had been requested. Fortunately for Charles Buchan, the court agreed and he was dismissed from the Bar. Highly dangerous substances such as opium were routinely sold over the counter in medicinal preparations around this time, and, unfortunately, it was not uncommon to see cases of accidental overdose in the courts.

Assault

A more frequent crime seen in the courts was that of assault, which often ended with the accused receiving a relatively lenient sentence in comparison to crimes of theft and dishonesty. In 1856, William Littlejohn was charged with assaulting two women, Elizabeth Nugent and Agnes Forbes, in a field within Kaime's Farm, St Ninian's. Having been found guilty by the jury, the court sentenced Littlejohn to eight days' imprisonment.

Alexander McIntyre, described as 'a powerful looking man', was also charged with assaulting his wife at their house in Baker Street in 1897. The indictment stated that McIntyre had:

[...]threw her down on the floor, trampled upon and kicked her, struck her repeatedly with a fire shovel and fender, threw her into the fireplace and burned her face, broke the bones of both her arms andone of her legs, her breastbone and one of her ribs, and cut off part of one of her fingers.

McIntyre, who had previously been convicted of a violent crime, pleaded not guilty and the case went to trial in the Stirling Circuit Court. Mrs McIntyre, who still had bandages on her head and showed signs of having sustained a violent attack, was the first to give evidence. She stated that on the day in question, her husband had gone out of the house after dinner, and shortly afterwards she also left the house 'to get some liquor'. She told the court that when she returned to the house, 'very much the worse of liquor', she fell against the fire and burned herself. Mrs McIntyre also said that she was not aware that her husband had touched her and woke up in the infirmary remembering nothing of the incident. She also said that her husband had warned her previously not to take any drink, but she had not listened to him. Mrs McIntyre's son, Alexander, was the next to give evidence, stating that on the day in question his father had returned home about four o'clock in the afternoon and went to sleep in his bed. He continued that he and his brother James had helped their mother home later in the day and that around six o'clock, she was lying bleeding. Young Alexander was particular in stressing to the court that his father did not assault his mother. The court, however, seeing through this attempt to cover up the brutal attack, presumably through their fear of Alexander McIntyre, found him guilty.

His Lordship, on passing sentence, made a point of stressing the brutality of the assault and highlighting that McIntyre had a number of previous convictions recorded against him. One such conviction had been in 1876, where he was sentenced to eight months' imprisonment for stabbing his first wife; another conviction in 1885 was for fracturing the bones of a person 'to the danger of their life', when he was imprisoned for eighteen months. His Lordship stated that he had a duty not to allow such a man to remain at large again and that he would ensure men and women were protected from him for many years to come'. Alexander McIntyre was sentenced to fourteen years' penal servitude.

A drunken brawl ended in Robert Wordie and Catherine Kane appearing before the court in 1903. The charge was that in a dwelling house in St Mary's Wynd, occupied by Wordie, they had assaulted Francis Kane in the lobby leading to the house. Accused of beating him with their fists and a poker, and of knocking

Kane down and killing him, the two accused pleaded not guilty to the charge. A number of witnesses were examined, who all spoke of a drunken brawl having taken place, and that Catherine Kane had been very active in the assault. After evidence had been heard, the original charge of culpable homicide was reduced to that of assault, to which both accused pleaded guilty. Counsel for the Crown decided that they would not press for a sentence upon Wordie and he was dismissed from the Bar. Lord Young, addressing Catherine Kane remarked that her 'language and actions showed that she intended to do harm to the man', and sentenced her to two months' imprisonment.

Fraud

Cases of fraud were often harshly dealt with by the courts in the nineteenth century. In 1863, Robert Duff had been brought from the prison of Stirling to face trial for 'fraudulently representing' to James Craig, a rag merchant in Spittal Street, that he was about to commence business as an auctioneer, valuer and commission agent in Striling. The circumstances were that Duff had told Craig that he had a quantity of ropes to sell, which he had been given by a relative who was the manager of a coal works. Having falsified documents which showed him as owning the quantity of rope mentioned, Duff obtained money from Craig on a promise that it would be delivered to him. Of course, the rope was never delivered to Craig, as Duff did not possess it in the first place. Having been found guilty, Duff was sentenced to three years' penal servitude.

Child Desertion

In light of the lack of reliable contraception available in the nineteenth century, and widespread poverty, crimes involving child desertion or child murder were, unfortunately, often seen by the courts. One particular case in 1874 involved a mother and daughter, Helen Telford and Margaret Telford. It appeared that a domestic servant named Elizabeth Davidson, who lived in Bridge of Allan, had entrusted her illegitimate child to the care of Helen Telford, giving her £2 to take the child. However, Helen and her daughter had sold the clothes, which had been provided for the child, finally leaving the three-month-old infant to perish on the public road between Pirnhall and Bannockburn, stripped of its clothes. Thankfully, the child was rescued and the heartless pair was brought to justice. Both mother and daughter were sentenced to seven years' penal servitude.

Bibliography

Books

Bland, James, *The Common Hangman: English and Scottish Hangmen Before the Abolition of Public Executions*, Zardoz Books (2nd revised edition, 2001)

Kinnaird, David, *Tales of the Stirling Ghostwalk* (self-published under creative commons license, 2009)

Livingston, Sheila, *Confess and be Hanged: Scottish Crime and Punishment Through the Ages*, Birlin Ltd, (Illustrated Edition, 1999)

Stirling's Talking Stones, Various Authors, Stirling Council Library Service

The Story of Stirling Old Town Jail, Souvenir Guide Book, Stirling District Tourism

Websites

NHS Forth Valley

Scottish Court Service

Scottish Law Online

The National Archives of Scotland

The Scottish Government

The *Stirling Journal* Archives

The *Stirling Observer* Archives

Victorian Crime and Punishment

www.instirling.com

www.stirling.gov.uk

www.sps.gov.uk

www.police-information.co.uk

www.archiveshub.ac.uk

Other titles published by The History Press

Auld Stirling Punishments

DAVID KINNAIRD

From the murder of James I and the brutal torture of his betrayers to the beheading of Radical Weavers Baird and Hardie, the history of crime and punishment in Stirling's Royal Burgh has reflected the passions and prejudices of the Scottish nation. Richly illustrated, and filled with victims and villains, nobles, executioners and torturers, this book explores Stirling's criminal heritage and the many grim and ancient punishments exacted inside the region's churches, workhouses and schools. It is a shocking survey of our nation's penal history.

978 0 7524 6019 2

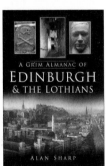

Scottish Bodysnatchers: A Gazetteer

GEOFF HOLDER

Graverobbing was a dark but profitable industry in pre-Victorian Scotland – criminals, gravediggers and middle-class medical students alike abstracted newly-buried corpses to send to the anatomy schools. Richly illustrated, filled with hundreds of stories of 'reanimated' corpses, daring thefts, and with Robert Louis Stevenson's classic short story *The Body Snatcher* at the end, this macabre guide will delight everyone who loves Scotland's dark past.

978 0 7524 5603 4

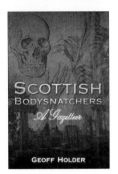

A Grim Almanac of Edinburgh & the Lothians

ALAN SHARP

Seldom in history has there been a city with a more sordid reputation than Edinburgh. Beneath the surface respectability of the jewel in the Scottish crown lies a warren of filth-ridden alleys and stairs where thieves, murderers and ghouls of every description planned and carried out their foul deeds. In this book we meet them all. Captain Porteous, the corrupt official who inspired the population to mob justice; and, worst of all, Mr Burke and Mr Hare, who plied their swift trade in corpses for the dissection table of Dr Knox.

978 0 7509 5105 0

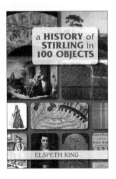

A History of Stirling in 100 Objects

ELSPETH KING

A History of the World in 100 Objects by the British Museum and the BBC is a project which has fired the public imagination throughout the land. *A History of Stirling in 100 Objects* is the first published tribute act, demonstrating that the local, the national and the international are always present, wherever the place, and that the World is where we live. Compiled by Elspeth King and with photography by Michael McGinnes, collections curator, this book will appeal to everyone interested in finding out more about Stirling through its material culture.

978 0 7524 5932 5

Visit our website and discover thousands of other History Press books.

www.thehistorypress.co.uk